Bilingualism

Bilingualism provides a concise and lively introduction to bilingualism as a social and linguistic phenomenon and explains its impact on individuals and on society. Addressing questions such as what it means to be bilingual, how one becomes bilingual, and how exposure to more than one language affects a child's cognitive development, this book features:

- an introduction to the linguistic, sociolinguistic, and cognitive outcomes of bilingualism, including bilingual language acquisition, the grammar of language-mixing, the link between language choice and identity, and the value of maintaining and promoting bilingualism;
- up-to-date overviews of the prominent concerns and facts about bilingualism;
- activities and discussion questions which invite readers to consider their own perspectives on bilingualism and how it manifests in their own lives and communities;
- links to relevant videos and suggested further reading, including topical novels, short stories, and essays.

Aimed at students with no background in linguistics, this book is essential reading for anyone studying bilingualism for the first time.

Shahrzad Mahootian is Professor Emerita in the Department of Linguistics, Northeastern Illinois University, USA.

Routledge Guides to Linguistics

Series Editor: Betty J. Birner is a Professor of Linguistics and Cognitive Science in the Department of English at Northern Illinois University.

Routledge Guides to Linguistics are a set of concise and accessible guidebooks which provide an overview of the fundamental principles of a subject area in a jargon-free and undaunting format. Designed for students of Linguistics who are approaching a particular topic for the first time, or students who are considering studying linguistics and are eager to find out more about it, these books will both introduce the essentials of a subject and provide an ideal springboard for further study.

This series is published in conjunction with the Linguistic Society of America. Founded in 1924 to advance the scientific study of language, the LSA plays a critical role in supporting and disseminating linguistic scholarship both to professional linguists and to the general public.

Titles in this series:

Sign Languages
Structures and Contexts
Joseph C. Hill, Diane C. Lillo-Martin and Sandra K. Wood

Language, Gender, and Sexuality
An Introduction
Scott F. Kiesling

Linguistics and Law
Jeffrey P. Kaplan

More information about this series can be found at www.routledge.com/series/RGL

Linguistic Society of America

Bilingualism

Shahrzad Mahootian

Routledge
Taylor & Francis Group

LONDON AND NEW YORK

First published 2020
by Routledge
2 Park Square, Milton Park, Abingdon, Oxon OX14 4RN

and by Routledge
52 Vanderbilt Avenue, New York, NY 10017

Routledge is an imprint of the Taylor & Francis Group, an informa business

British Library Cataloguing-in-Publication Data
A catalogue record for this book is available from the British Library

Library of Congress Cataloging-in-Publication Data
A catalog record has been requested for this book

ISBN: 978-0-8153-7010-9 (hbk)
ISBN: 978-0-8153-7011-6 (pbk)
ISBN: 978-1-351-25076-4 (ebk)

Typeset in Times New Roman
by Deanta Global Publishing Services, Chennai, India

To Amber and Leila, future bilinguals

Contents

Acknowledgments

I would like to express my sincere thanks and appreciation to Lewis Gebhardt, Judith Kaplan-Weinger, and Erin Marks for all of their great suggestions and editorial advice as they read through "a few" drafts of this book. I'm also extremely grateful for the encouragement and support they provided throughout.

Special and abundant thanks to Sonya Chen, Hanadi Elmanaseer, Heyli Gomez, and Jade Newton for providing and reviewing some of the codeswitched data and explanations, and for their enthusiasm in doing so. My gratitude extends to the series editor, Betty Birner, for her guidance, eagle-eye editing, and her shared love of commas.

Chapter 1

Introduction

Do you or does someone you know speak more than one language? Have you ever thought about how one becomes bilingual? Have you wondered why some people can speak more than one language easily and fluently while others struggle in learning and using other languages? In this volume, we consider many aspects of this extraordinarily ordinary human capacity—that of acquiring and using multiple languages. Bilingualism has long been an area of interest and study in a number of fields, from linguistics to psychology to education. It has been defined from many perspectives: social, structural, cognitive, historical, legal, and educational. Many of the definitions and discussions intertwine and overlap, yet each discipline focuses on specific aspects and functions of bilingualism. As a subfield of linguistics, as with all things in linguistics, the focus of bilingualism is to look for patterns in form and function: to look for rule-governed, systematic generalizations that guide the grammatical features of bilingualism as well as the functional aspects of language use by bilinguals. Whether exploring the grammar of utterances produced by mixing two or more languages, or looking at the social functions of choosing one language over another in bilingual speakers' repertoires, we will see that bilinguals' language use and choices, like monolinguals', are complex and rule-driven. Our starting point in the exploration of this topic is to identify what a bilingual is, and how bilingualism comes to be.

Thinking Matters

Before reading further, take a moment to consider how nations, communities, and individuals become bilingual.

Simply, bilingualism is a result of languages in contact—or more precisely, the result of people, cultures, and/or nations in contact. Contact can come in many forms, with migration, war, and colonization as the top contact-producing events historically. Consequently, many countries have come to house multiple languages. For example, there are 67 languages spoken in Iran. Papua New Guinea has the rest of the world beat, housing 841 languages, including 3 official languages, among a population of approximately 7 million. In Papua New Guinea, virtually everyone is conversant in two or more languages.

Political and economic alliances and the often arbitrary assignment of national borders can present opportunities for bilingual communities to develop. Switzerland is the oft-cited example of alliances and borders leading to four languages—Swiss German, French, Italian, and Romansch—having official status. However, other major reasons for the existence of multilingual countries include colonization and immigration (often to escape war, persecution, or economic upheaval). In the United States, for example, linguistic diversity can be mostly attributed to immigration, beginning with Spanish explorers in the 15th and 16th centuries and followed by the British beginning in the 17th century. In the 18th, 19th, and early 20th centuries, Germans, Celts, Italians, Chinese, and immigrants from Slavic countries found their way to the United States (US). As a consequence of world events in which the United States was either directly or indirectly involved, the mid- and late-20th century into the 2000s saw more immigrants from Asian and Middle Eastern countries seeking refuge or better lives in the United States.[1]

Other sources of contact include educational and career opportunities, commerce, and tourism, which can result in the acquisition of languages at an individual level rather than at a community or national level. Consequently, bilingualism can develop during childhood, as part of the cultural transmission of language within a family and/or a bilingual community, or during adulthood. If you are thinking, then, that bilingualism is not a new trend, or a trend at all, you are absolutely correct. In fact, more than half of the world's population is bilingual, able to use more than one language on a regular basis. That said, we set as the goal of this chapter an overview of decades-long efforts involved in defining bilingualism, and the factors that need to be considered in describing the bilingual individual.

In Chapter 2, we look at bilingualism and multilingualism on a global scale and discover that many nations have been bilingual, officially (*de jure*) or unofficially (*de facto*), for millennia. Overall, the story that unfolds is one where bilingualism is not the exception, but for over 50% of the world's population it is the norm. We also take a closer look at the complex relationships between and across languages in contact situations and examine how the variety of languages available to an individual or speech community is employed as a resource in social interactions and as a means for self-identification and community membership. The flipside of contact between cultures and languages—how contact, in some cases, contributes to linguistic and cultural endangerment—will also be discussed.

Chapter 3 examines borrowing, language mixing, and codeswitching, the most common linguistic by-products of bilingualism. We review the various models that have been proposed to explain how the bilingual's two grammars interact to produce mixed language utterances (codeswitches), and we explore the social functions of codeswitching and language choice. In Chapter 4, we take a look at how children become bilingual and whether being raised bilingually affects the natural developmental path of language acquisition. Moreover, we examine the implications of language mixing in the speech of young children and the age at which they start to differentiate between their two or more languages. In Chapter 5, we consider the cognitive effects of bilingualism, including theories of how language may be organized in the bilingual brain and how bilingualism may affect intelligence. Chapter 6 summarizes the main points presented in this volume and offers concluding remarks.

1.1 What is Bilingualism and Who is Bilingual?

The practice of using two or more languages has earned a number of titles, and even more definitions. Of course 'bilingualism' specifically refers to the ability to use two languages, but most linguists use the terms *bilingualism*, *multilingualism*, and more recently, *plurilingualism*, to capture what more than half the world's population considers a normal part of their lives and identities. In this volume, we use the three terms more or less interchangeably to refer to the same linguistic phenomenon, that of the coexistence of two or more languages, whether to refer to bilingual individuals or communities or nations. The latter two terms best apply to contexts where there are two or more languages and/or distinct dialects (varieties)[2] present in a community without the expectation that all members of the community know or use all the languages. *Bilingual*, on the other hand, can best describe individuals who have the capability of using more than one language or dialect. But what do we mean when we remark that someone is bilingual or claim that we ourselves are? Or that someone is not bilingual? In his article "Multilingualism: Some Central Concepts," John Edwards (2013, p. 5) asks, "Where does bilingualism 'start'? And how are we to accommodate different levels of fluency?" We shall see that both questions continue to elicit a variety of answers, leading us to conclude that a one-size-fits-all definition of bilingualism is not the answer.

Thinking Matters

Take a moment to write down a definition starting with "To be bilingual", and then share your definition with others. Did you agree with one another?

As you may have discovered, everyone has a general idea of what it means to be bilingual, whether they themselves are bilingual or not. As noted previously, at the most elementary level, we think of a bilingual as someone with the ability to use two (or more) languages. But how do we define use? For example, a speaker may be completely fluent in Language A when talking about car engines but quite at a loss when it comes to naming common flowers and trees in Language A. Or the bilingual may be able to read and write in one of his or her two languages, but not in both. Are both or either of these individuals bilingual? Moreover, definitions of individual bilingualism only partially overlap with definitions of bilingualism at a national level, thus requiring other measures and terms of reference to cover and distinguish each. In this section, the focus will be on determining which linguistic variables are relevant to forming a practicable definition of bilingualism.

To get us started, consider the following scenarios and decide whether you would describe the speaker in each to be bilingual. Make note of the reasons for your judgments. Which of the scenarios did the definition you wrote cover?

1. The bank teller who provides service to English-speaking and Spanish-speaking customers in each of their respective languages. Yes___ No____ Maybe__. Why?

2. The teacher in a bilingual elementary school classroom who speaks English with a noticeable Urdu accent. Yes___ No____ Maybe__. Why?

3. The four-year-old child raised in a Senegalese-French dual language household who occasionally utters sentences using words from both languages. Yes___ No____ Maybe__. Why?

4. The annoyed teenager raised in a dual language household who, when spoken to in Greek, will respond only in English. Yes___ No____ Maybe__. Why?

5. The college student who has studied Chinese for three years in preparation for an exchange program where all classes will be in Chinese. Yes___ No____ Maybe__. Why?

6. The server in a trendy Barcelona tapas bar who regularly speaks in English to English-speaking tourists. Yes___ No____ Maybe__. Why?

7. The adult who can converse comfortably on a variety of topics in two languages, but can only read and write in one of the languages. Yes___ No____ Maybe__. Why?

8. The international student from Saudi Arabia who is finishing her second year in an MA program in the US with a 3.5 GPA. Yes___ No____ Maybe__. Why?

9. The second-generation Vietnamese-American college freshman who uses Vietnamese and English frequently at home, at school and at his part-time job, but can only read and write in English. Yes___ No____ Maybe__. Why?

Did you find any commonalities across the nine scenarios that swayed you toward a 'yes', 'no', or 'maybe' answer for each? It would not be surprising if you thought this exercise to be less than straightforward, whether you are monolingual or multilingual. The bank teller, the sulky teenager, the college student, the Vietnamese-American freshman, and even the four-year-old, along with all the others, are unequivocally bilinguals. However, for some people, the ability to read and write in both languages, to have native-like command of both languages, and keeping the two languages separate and unmixed, may be nonnegotiable defining features of bilinguals. It's important to note that, as linguists, we recognize that 'balanced bilinguals', speakers with equal abilities in all of their languages, are rare. Or more accurately, that they are an ideal, based on the mistaken notion that a bilingual is simply two monolinguals in one body: someone who has attained the same advanced linguistic and cultural knowledge along with equal academic knowledge and literacy skills in all of their languages. So what does it mean to be bilingual? In the following sections we will try our best to answer this complex question by reviewing existing definitions and perspectives.

1.2 Defining Bilingualism

The older, monolingual, view of bilingualism has had many negative consequences, one of the worst being that many bilinguals are very critical of their own language competence and do not consider themselves to be bilingual.

(François Grosjean, 2002)[3]

Though the earliest definitions of bilingualism emphasized "native-like control" and equal fluency in both languages (Bloomfield, 1933, p. 56), throughout the literature we can also find more general definitions. For example, Uriel Weinreich defined bilingualism as "the practice of alternately using two languages" (1953, p. 1). François Grosjean's bilinguals are speakers "who use two or more languages (or dialects) in their everyday lives" (2010, p. 4). Although both Weinreich's and Grosjean's definitions are somewhat fuzzy, they are useful nonetheless because they are so general and allow for the inclusion and gradation of the many factors—as you noted in the previous exercise—that are inherently involved in defining bilingualism and determining who is and who isn't a bilingual. At this time, linguists and scholars from other fields largely agree that a single definition cannot capture the varieties of ways one can be bilingual. Nor can a single definition address the fluidity of language capabilities that a single bilingual experiences. Like the example mentioned earlier, one can be completely at ease while discussing engine parts in one language (LA), but not in the other (LB), and conversely, be quite knowledgeable when naming the varieties of wild flowers in a field in LB but not in LA.

Take a moment to think about your own language experiences and consider the following questions: Have you studied a language through an exchange program, or through language classes, or through online courses? How old were you? How well do you think you learned the language? What gave you the most trouble—speaking, listening, grammar, pronunciation? How much of the language do you remember/use now? Research that has asked these types of questions has helped us to understand both the subtle and the obvious differences resulting from when and how speakers have learned their languages. Linguists and other scholars have a fairly strong consensus on six factors they believe influence individuals' bilingual capabilities:

(a) age of acquisition—whether the languages were acquired in early childhood, adolescence, or learned in adulthood
(b) manner of acquisition—whether the languages were acquired in a natural setting, such as in one's home, or in a formal setting, such as in school or in language classes
(c) sequence of acquisition—whether the languages were acquired *simultaneously* or *sequentially*
(d) literacy skills—whether the individual can read and write in any or all of their languages
(e) function—whether the individual's languages are used for the same purposes, in the same domains, and with the same degree of regularity
(f) fluency—whether the individual has equal linguistic capabilities in all of their languages

Now, let's look at each of the six factors and consider how they may affect one's degree of bilingualism.

Age of acquisition—There are as many ways to achieve bilingualism as there are definitions of bilingualism. To start, we separate out childhood bilingualism from bilingualism attained in adulthood. It has long been thought that the optimal period to acquire multiple languages is during childhood, and more specifically, between two years of age and puberty. In fact, initially, it was hypothesized that this period was a 'critical period' for language acquisition because of the important developmental changes children's brains go through from birth to puberty (Penfield and Roberts, 1959, Lenneberg, 1967). It was further hypothesized that language acquisition capabilities decline dramatically after puberty and that speakers exposed to language after this period would not achieve full mastery of the grammatical systems of the target language. This theory, which was initially proposed to address first language acquisition and later extended to second language acquisition, has not been without controversy, especially in the context of second language acquisition. The issues under debate include the validity of the timeline for first language acquisition, i.e., whether puberty is the ceiling after which language acquisition becomes more effortful, whether all components of language are equally susceptible to the same 'critical period', and finally, whether a 'critical period' exists when acquiring a second, third, etc. language.

Over the last half century, first and second language research has brought more clarity to the issues surrounding the existence of a critical period for first and multiple language acquisition. One outcome has been to put aside the term "critical period" and instead adopt the terms *optimal* or *sensitive* period. A second outcome has been to look at the acquisition process of the various components of language (e.g., sounds [phonology], grammatical rules [syntax], and words [lexicon]) independently of each other. For the purposes of this volume, we will restrict our focus to second/multiple language acquisition studies. Research results in this area neither fully support nor refute a sensitive/optimal period, though the ability to master some aspects of a second language lessens with age and takes more effort. For example, our ability to perceive and produce sounds that are not part of our home language(s) suffers as we age, with the greatest decline appearing after age 17 (Kuhl, 2014).

In a recent study of 669,498 native and non-native speakers of English, Hartshorne, Tenenbaum, and Pinker (2018) found that grammar-learning abilities also change with age. The focus of their research was on adult second language learners' abilities to acquire syntax (knowledge of the rules of grammar). Specifically, they sought to answer why adult second language learners don't attain the same level of grammatical proficiency as adult native speakers of the target language, or those who have learned their second language in childhood. They determined that there is an optimal period for acquiring grammatical rules but that it is between 17 and 18 years of age, much later than previously hypothesized. They concluded that grammar-learning ability is

> preserved almost to the crux of adulthood (17.4 years old) and then declines steadily. This finding held not only for "difficult" syntactic phenomena but also for "easy" syntactic phenomena that are normally mastered early in acquisition. The results support the existence of a sharply defined critical period for language acquisition, but the age of offset is much later than previously speculated.
>
> (p. 263)

It should be noted that Hartshorne et al.'s conclusions pertain solely to grammar and that they do not use the term "critical period" as a developmental span of time with an end point for learning another language. Rather, the term is used to describe a period after which the adult second language learner respondents in their survey show "diminished achievement … whatever its cause". They add:

> There is little consensus as to whether children's advantage comes from superior neural plasticity [as hypothesized by Lenneberg], an earlier start that gives them additional years of learning, limitations in cognitive processing that prevent them from being distracted by irrelevant information, a lack of interference from a well-learned first language, a greater willingness to experiment and make errors, a greater desire to conform to their peers, or a greater likelihood of learning through immersion in a community of native speakers.
>
> (p. 263)

To be clear, no studies of multiple language acquisition claim that there is a point at which a second, third, fourth, etc., language cannot be learned. Rather, Hartshorne et al.'s and other researchers' studies indicate that languages learned at various ages will result in various levels of fluency. Consequently, in defining bilingualism we need to consider age as a factor. The age factor alone pushes us toward proposing definitions of bilingualism that are gradable and situated on a continuum rather than striving for a single monolithic definition.

Manner of acquisition and **sequence of acquisition** are closely tied. Whether the languages are acquired in a natural setting without any formal teaching involved, such as through growing up in a bilingual household, or in a formal setting, such as in language classes, will affect the ease and rate of acquisition as well as fluency. These two factors are intertwined with age of acquisition. Often, when both languages are learned in childhood, they are acquired at the same time, or *simultaneously*. However, it is also possible for a child to acquire a second or other language *sequentially*; for example, in cases where the home language differs from the school or majority language, children are (mostly) exposed to and use the home language until they start school and acquire the other language. Typically, *early bilingualism* (before age seven) has its start in the home, with infants simultaneously exposed to more than one language by their caregivers. Early bilingualism can also result from the young child attending a preschool where the language used by teachers differs from the home language. In this scenario, as with the home situation, the child is exposed to two or more languages regularly during the critical language acquisition period, more or less in a simultaneous manner. Languages acquired sequentially, if not acquired during early childhood, are often learned in formal classroom settings—for example, in high school foreign language classes, or later in adulthood, whether formally through language classes or other means.

We come now to the fourth factor, **literacy skills**. Although an important feature of education, literacy is not considered a linguistics issue, per se. Linguistics as a field is primarily interested in how language works as a system of rules within and across speech communities. Specifically, linguists are interested in spoken language: what is said and what isn't said by speakers, how language is structured, how it varies in form and use among speakers and communities, in what ways languages are similar to each other, and in what ways they differ from one another. Linguists are also interested in how spoken languages are acquired, how languages change over time, and how language is processed in the brain, among many other things. Ethnologue estimates that of the 7,097 languages in the world, "3,188 are likely unwritten", about half of them (www.ethnologue.com/enterprise-faq/how-many-languages-world-are-unwritten-0). Since linguists are primarily interested in spoken language, the ability to read and write doesn't figure into whether someone is considered bilingual. That is, someone can be bilingual yet non-literate in (any of) the languages they speak. Just as we would not expect a monolingual to be literate in order to include them as a member of a speech community, we apply the same standards for speakers of more than one language—literacy is not a requirement of their bilingualism, just as literacy is not a requirement of monolingualism. However, literacy can be a factor in what *type* of bilingual the speaker may be. In Section 1.3, we consider various combinations of the six factors, and how they interact to produce different types of bilinguals.

You may wonder why a discussion of **function** is necessary for the definition of bilingualism. How often and for what functions speakers use each language is an indication of the status and vitality of each language within the community. Understanding the relationship of languages in a speech community can also serve as a predictive tool for language loss and endangerment. It should come as no surprise that bilinguals do not randomly choose which language to use where and with whom, or when it is acceptable to mix the languages to produce codeswitched speech. For the bilingual, each language has its own bundle of functions and **domains** of use that are governed by the norms of the speech communities to which the speakers belong. Among these domains are family, religion, education, employment, and friendship. In each domain, one language is socially expected and (viewed as more) acceptable (Fishman, Cooper, Newman, & Ma, 1971). The language you choose to use in each domain is further governed by internal dynamics. For example, for the immigrant family, the home language—the language associated with the speakers' ethnicity and culture—is commonly expected to be used in the home. However, different family members may be more or less insistent on this language preference. It is more typical for older family members, such as grandparents, to expect the home language to be used in the home than for younger family members to expect this.

Thinking Matters

Bilinguals: Consider the five domains of family, religion, education, employment, and friendship mentioned previously. Which language is predominant in which domain(s) in your bilingual community?

Monolinguals: Consider the same five domains. In which domains do you think the majority language is considered the norm, and in which would bilinguals' other language be expected?

In addition to audience and where the conversation is taking place, the topic of conversation will also determine which language will be used—even if it is not the language usually used in that domain. To expand the family example, in the same scenario, if all members are bilingual, it would be normal and acceptable to use the public language (the dominant language used outside of the home for education, work, and general services) to talk about technical aspects of one's work or studies.

Possibly the most elusive factor in formulating a definition of bilingualism is speakers' degree of **fluency** in each language. The elusiveness stems partly from the fact that there isn't an agreed-upon measure for fluency, on the one hand, while on the other, it's not clear exactly which components should be measured to ascertain fluency. Perhaps more to the point is to ask what can/should we reasonably expect from speakers in order to pronounce them bilingual, to definitively distinguish the bilingual from the non-bilingual (i.e., the monolingual or the language learner, the phrase book user)? Does fluency mean native-like language performance? Or does it mean communicative competence, the ability to understand and to be understood?

Native-like pronunciation is often considered another sign of language knowledge and fluency. But consider the individual who has moved to another country as an adult, is employed as a professor in a university, and yet after years of living there continues to speak the second language with an accent and makes some grammatical errors in that language. He or she has no difficulties understanding the language and communicating with colleagues and students, and they don't have difficulty understanding him or her. How should we measure this speaker's fluency? It stands to reason that fluency, like bilingualism, is best treated as a moving target, a bundle of features that may be combined in a variety of ways to produce a competent communicator, though not always a "native" speaker in all features.[4] In fact, some have suggested using **proficiency** rather than fluency as a variable. Proficiency implies that the speaker may not be native-like but is able to perform various language tasks easily at various levels (for example, a speaker may have beginner level proficiency to perform some tasks such as delivering a lecture in their other language[s] but have high proficiency in conducting everyday conversations with friends, during shopping, or even *understanding* academic lectures). Subsequently, proficiency can be measured either as a set of linguistic structure tasks (speaker's knowledge of grammatical rules and sounds for example, i.e., linguistic competence) or as tasks that measure the speaker's ability to meet speech community expectations and norms in a native-like manner (i.e., linguistic performance). The former approach is known as a criterion-based evaluation, the latter as norm-based. Not surprisingly, a third approach has been suggested, a process-based approach which measures and takes into account both competence (knowledge of rules) and performance to determine speakers' proficiency in their other language(s).

One last factor that is more complicated and subjective than a measure of fluency is that of **self-assessment**. When bilinguals are asked why they consider themselves to be bilingual, they often reply that they are "comfortable" using their languages in (almost) all contexts. They often remark that they feel comfortable interacting with bilingual and monolingual individuals from each of the related cultures and that they also feel accepted as an equal member of those communities and cultures. Not surprisingly, this attitude and sense of comfort and belonging is most often described by early bilinguals (see next section), and less often by late bilinguals (see next section). In fact, many late bilinguals who have acquired their other languages formally through language classes make a distinction between their ability to use the language competently and their ability to use the language appropriately within the culture, including understanding and making jokes, using colloquial/everyday language, and using idioms.

1.3 Types of Bilinguals

Along the way to developing the best definition of bilingualism, a number of categories or types of bilingualism have been identified by various researchers (Hoffman, 1991; Edwards, 2013; among others). These categories have some overlap and, not surprisingly, correlate with the six described earlier. Some focus on the age of exposure to two or more languages, while others consider the context of acquisition (natural or formal). Still others are concerned with the performance of the bilingual and the functions speakers can perform in each of their languages.

1.3.1 By Age

- *Early bilingualism*—As the name suggests, this occurs when the child is exposed to more than one language anytime from birth to puberty, during the sensitive period for language acquisition. Some linguists, psycholinguists, and language acquisition researchers believe that a finer cut should be made to distinguish those children exposed to multiple languages in the first few years of life (up to about five or six years of age) from those exposed to their other languages later in childhood, but before puberty. This reasoning springs from a distinction between simultaneous acquisition in a natural home environment and sequential acquisition in a formal, educational setting. It's reasonable to assume that there may very well be some linguistic, social, and cognitive advantages in each case, but there isn't any concrete evidence in either direction.
- *Late bilingualism*—This term captures bilingualism that is achieved after the sensitive period, and after the first language has been fully acquired. Late bilingualism would necessarily take place outside of the home, most often in an educational or work setting. For example, high schoolers who have immigrated with their parents and have acquired the language of the new community would be considered late bilinguals, as would the parents if they, too, acquired the language.

1.3.2 By Method

- *Primary bilingualism*—Edwards (2013) describes this as "dual competence acquired naturally through contextual demands".

Although this definition can overlap with that of early bilingualism, it can also apply to late bilinguals.

* *Secondary bilingualism*—Like late bilingualism, this refers to linguistic competence acquired through formal instruction.
* *Elite bilingualism*—Also called *elective bilingualism*, elite bilingualism usually involves two or more prestige languages. Often the elected language is learned formally in an educational setting. The language(s) chosen will naturally differ from one nation to the next and may also change over time. For example, at one time, in the West, French and Latin were the prestige languages no intellectual could do without. Today, English is considered a prestige language in most, if not all, corners of the world.

1.3.3 By Function

* *Receptive (passive) bilingualism*—This label is meant to account for those bilinguals who can understand a language when it is spoken to them (or in written form), but cannot (easily) speak it. Receptive bilingualism is often an outcome of language learning that takes place in adulthood and in classroom settings. Often the learner doesn't have the opportunity to use the language outside of the classroom. However, receptive bilingualism can also come about in childhood, in bilingual households. The child may decide that one language is sufficient to fulfill his/her communication needs with family, friends, and the larger community outside of his home and family, and 'save' the other language for times he/she needs to understand speakers of the other language.
* *Productive (active) bilingualism*—Productive bilinguals can both understand and produce each of their languages. Typically, they use both languages frequently and in a variety of contexts.
* *Additive bilingualism*—Generally, this term describes late and/or secondary bilinguals who are able to acquire a new language while maintaining their first language, hence adding the new language to their linguistic resources.
* *Subtractive bilingualism*—The opposite of additive bilingualism, the term captures bilingual speakers who, for a variety of

reasons, have replaced one language with another. Typically, their first or home language is replaced with the language that is perceived to be more dominant or valued in the larger speech community. This is not uncommon, and is characteristic of the third- or even the second-generation offspring of immigrants. We will look at this and other occurrences of language shift in more depth in Chapter 2.

Achieved bilingualism—Like elective bilingualism, achieved bilingualism is accomplished through formal education. Like elective bilingualism, speakers learn a status language associated with a higher social status. In the case of achieved bilingualism, the chosen language also holds the promise of more career options than does the native language. For example, in many countries, the choice of English as a second language (rather than a language used in the region, or Spanish or French), reflects the status of English as an academic language and also as a resource in non-academic global contexts such as travel, entertainment, and commerce.

Table 1.1 presents the relationship of types of bilingualism to some of the crucial factors discussed in this chapter that play into the acquisition of two or more languages. For example, in reading the chart you see that primary bilinguals are speakers who may have acquired their languages at any time during or after the sensitive period either simultaneously or sequentially.

Table 1.1 Types of bilinguals by age and sequence of learning languages

Type	During sensitive period	Post-sensitive period	Simultaneous	Sequential
Early	X		X	
Primary	X	X	X	X
Late	X	X		X
Secondary		X		X
Receptive		X		X
Productive	X	X	X	X
Additive	X	X	X	X
Subtractive		X		X

1.4 Summary

In this chapter, we laid the groundwork for looking further into this rich area of linguistics and for understanding bilingualism as a natural part of the capabilities of humans and of human societies. Given the variations in age of acquisition, method of acquisition, and function of each language, speakers may display varying degrees of ability and dominance in each of their languages in different contexts. They may also possess different degrees of literacy skills or none at all. Though it's taken a few decades, linguists and scholars in other fields have come to agree that bilingualism, as with any communicative practice, is dynamic and varies within and across speakers, and is, in the end, best represented on a continuum. It is safe to say, given the variables that need to be factored in, that no one definition will suffice to fit all bilinguals. In fact, the multiple factors that need to be considered make a single definition impractical and inadequate. Instead, we adopt a definition which is more of a description, one which has the flexibility needed to capture the different types of bilinguals.

Discussion Questions and Projects

1. Use the Ethnologue website (www.ethnologue.com/) to answer the following questions:
   a. How many languages are there in the world?
   b. In terms of numbers of speakers, what are the top ten languages spoken in the world?
2. Use the US Census website (UScensus.org) to answer the next three questions:
   a. How many people in the US speak a language other than English?
   b. What are the top five languages spoken where you live?
   c. What percentage of respondents speaks Spanish as a home language?
3. Choose four countries from the CIA Factbook webpage at www. cia.gov/library/publications/the-world-factbook/fields/2098.html. How do the political, ethnic, and religious histories of these countries explain the presence of their various language communities?

4. *Group project*. Work with three or four other students to produce a mini-corpus of answers to the question: "What is bilingualism?" Begin with each student in your group asking five people in their circle of friends and family to define bilingualism. Then, bring the answers back to the group and pool them together to form a mini-corpus to be analyzed for patterns of similarities and differences in the words used to describe bilingualism. For a more robust corpus, pool the answers from all the groups in your class to analyze. Key terms to look for: speak, understand, use, read, write, fluent, native.

5. Read this opinion article by Dr. Gabrielle Hogan-Brun, Senior Research Fellow in the School of Education at the University of Bristol. Then, write a brief reply to indicate whether and why you agree or disagree with her perspective on multilingualism. www.swissinfo.ch/eng/multilingualism_switzerland-s-unique-selling-point/42890736.

Notes

1 Some examples include the Korean and Vietnam wars, and the Iranian Revolution.

2 I will be using the terms *dialect* and *variety* interchangeably throughout.

3 In response to interview questions asked on bilingualism by Judit Navracsics, Veszprem University, Hungary (February 2002).

4 Anecdotally, whenever I visit my relatives in Iran, they are always (seemingly) amazed by and compliment me on my maintained fluency in Persian (even though it's my first language!), remarking on my vocabulary and lack of hesitation in finding words despite the fact that I've lived in the US for decades. They are, however, quick to correct my Americanized pronunciation of 'r' and 'l' sounds in the beginning and middle of Persian words.

References and Recommended Readings

Bloomfield, L. (1933). *Language*. New York: Holt.

Crystal, D. (2003). *English as a Global Language*, 2nd edition. Cambridge, UK: Cambridge University Press.

Edwards, J. (2013). Multilingualism: Some central concepts. In: Bhatia, T., & Ritchie, W., (eds), *The Handbook of Bilingualism and Multilingualism*, 2nd edition (pp. 5–25). Malden, MA: Blackwell Publishers, Ltd.

Ethnologue, 21st edition, www.ethnologue.com/enterprise-faq/how-many-languages-world-are-unwritten-0.

European Union Commission Special Eurobarometer 386 Report: Europeans and Their languages (2012). ec.europa.eu/commfrontoffice/publicopinion/archives/ebs/ebs_386_en.pdf.

Fishman, J.A., Cooper, R., Newman, L., & Ma, R. (1971). *Bilingualism in the Barrio*. Bloomington, IN: Indiana University.

Grosjean, F. (2010). *Bilingual Life and Reality*. Cambridge, MA: Harvard University Press.

Grosjean, F. (2002). Interview. *The Bilingual Family Newsletter.* 19(4): 4–7.

Hartshorne, J.K., Tenenbaum, J.B., & Pinker, S. (2018). A critical period for second language acquisition: Evidence from 2/3 million English speakers. *Cognition.* 177: 263–277. doi: 10.1016/j.cognition.2018.04.007.

Haugen, E. (1953). *The Norwegian Language in America: A Study of Bilingual Behavior*. Philadelphia, PA: University of Pennsylvania Press.

Hoffman, C. (1991). *An Introduction to Bilingualism*. New York and London, UK: Longman.

Kuhl, P. (2014). The linguistics genius of babies. www.ted.com/talks/patricia_kuhl_the_linguistic_genius_of_babies (Retrieved July 20, 2018).

Lenneberg, E.H. (1967). *Biological Foundations of Language*. New York: Wiley.

Penfield, W., & Roberts, L. (1959). *Speech and Brain Mechanisms*. Princeton, NJ: Princeton University Press and London, UK: Oxford University Press.

Rumbaut, R.G., & Massey, D.S. (2013). Immigration and language diversity in the United States. *Daedalus.* 142(3): 141–154. www.ncbi.nlm.nih.gov/pmc/articles/PMC4092008/ (Retrieved July 28, 2018).

Weinreich, U. (1953). *Languages in Contact, Findings and Problems*. New York: Linguistic Circle of New York.

Chapter 2

Societal Bilingualism/ Plurilingualism

With more than half the population of the world using two or more languages, bilingualism is far from a rare or new phenomenon. Evidence of multilingual societies tells a story of social and linguistic contact stretching back two and a half millennia: from inscriptions left in stone by Persian and Egyptian dynasties to Anglo-Saxon England leases issued by Oswald bishop of Worcester containing switches between Latin and Old English (Schendl & Wright, 2012). From various documents we know that, throughout history, each conquest brought with it the language of the conquerors. The new language often became the court language, the language of government and law, leaving the local language(s) to be used as the everyday-life language(s).

These multilingual documents provide a window into the use of multiple languages to boast, to record, to inform, and to bind nations together. Stone columns in Persepolis and reliefs on mountainsides in Kermanshah, Iran, from 522–486 BC show inscriptions in three languages—Old Persian, Elamite, and Babylonian—describing the conquests of King Darius the Great. Likewise, the Rosetta Stone, circa 196 BC, is inscribed in two languages using three scripts: the "language of the gods" (Egyptian hieroglyphs), the "language of documents" (Egyptian demotic script), and Greek as used by the Ptolemaic government (Ray, 2007). The inscriptions on the Stone are a proclamation "issued in Egypt that praises Ptolemy V for his achievements and states that a statue will be set up in his honour" with further 'important dates' serving as reminders that festivals will be held and sacrifices will be made to celebrate Ptolemy's birthday and coronation (arch aeologymuseum.ca/the-rosetta-stone/).

One might argue that texts with translations in multiple languages, such as the inscriptions found in Iran or on the Rosetta Stone, are just that—translations. However, that the translations coexist on the same slab of stone provides evidence of societal bilingualism, and acknowledgment of more than one official language. The mix of Latin and Old English in the Anglo-Saxon leases indicates an even more widespread bilingualism among individuals.

Today, as in the past, many nations are plurilingual as a result of some sort of contact such as war, colonization, and immigration. There are approximately 7,090 languages spoken across 228 nations (ethnologue.com), and it is estimated that more than half the world's population uses two or more languages as part of their everyday life. For example, according to the European Commission's 2012 study and report of Europeans and their languages, over half of Europeans (54%) are conversant in more than one language, with 25% of those speakers able to speak at least two additional languages and 10% able to hold conversations in at least three additional languages (ec.europa .eu/commfrontoffice/publicopinion/archives/). In India, with 445 languages, nearly 30% of the over 1.3 billion members of the population speaks two or more languages. According to the US Census Bureau's 2013–2017 American Community Survey 5-Year Estimates, there are more than 350 languages spoken in the US, and approximately 20% of the age 5 and over population of 301,150,892 is bilingual. And as mentioned in Chapter 1, Papua New Guinea holds the world title for the most number of languages in one country. Nearly every one of the 7 million members of the population there speaks two or more languages—some combination of the 840 Indigenous languages (see Section 2.4 for a detailed definition of the term 'Indigenous language') and 1 non-Indigenous language (English) that are spread unevenly across 600 islands. In truth, there are no exclusively monolingual nations per se, although Japan and Iceland are often identified as such. In the case of the former, the Ainu, Japan's Indigenous population in northern Japan, speak Ainu, a language unrelated to Japanese or any other known language. Iceland is likely the most monolingual, with only two language systems, spoken and signed Icelandic.

Thinking Matters

Want more language facts? Look them up! Find out which 20 countries house 80% of the world's languages. Which languages have more than 100 million speakers?

We know, more or less, what it means for an individual to be bilingual/plurilingual, but what does it mean when we say a nation is? At the national level, bilingualism simply means that there is more than one linguistic population in the country. It does not mean, however, that the population of the country uniformly speaks more than one language—although in some cases this is true. In fact, a large percentage of the population may be monolingual, as is the case of the US, with only 20% of the population claiming to know more than one language, despite the fact that more than 350 languages are spoken in the US. Although many in the US believe that bilingualism is a new phenomenon, a quick jog through history tells us otherwise. Rumbaut and Massey (2013, p. 141) write,

> The United States historically has been a polyglot nation containing a diverse array of languages. At the time of independence, non-English European immigrants made up one quarter of the population and in Pennsylvania two-fifths of the population spoke German. In addition, an unknown but presumably significant share of the new nation's inhabitants spoke an American Indian or African language, suggesting that perhaps a third or more of all Americans spoke a language other than English. With the Louisiana Purchase in 1803 (which doubled the size of the country), the Treaty of 1818 with Britain (which added the Oregon Country), the Adams-Onís Treaty of 1819 with Spain (which gave Florida to the U.S.), and the Treaty of Guadalupe Hidalgo in 1848 (which acquired nearly half of Mexico), tens of thousands of French and Spanish speakers along with many more slaves and the diverse Indigenous peoples of those vast territories were added to the linguistic mix. Alaska and Hawaii would follow before the end of the 19th century.

While conquest and slavery clearly played a role in the 18th and 19th centuries, language diversity in the US since then has been driven primarily by immigration. Germans and Celts entered in large numbers in the 1840s and 1850s, followed after the Civil War by Scandinavians in the 1870s and 1880s and then by Slavs, Jews, and Italians from the 1880s to the first decades of the 20th century. According to the 1910 US Census, of the national population of 92 million, 10 million immigrants reported a mother tongue other than English or Celtic (Irish, Scottish, Welsh). Included in the 10 million, were 2.8 million speakers of German, 1.4 million speakers of Italian, 1.1 million speakers of Yiddish, 944,000 speakers of Polish, 683,000 speakers of Swedish, 529,000 speakers of French, 403,000 speakers of Norwegian, and 258,000 speakers of Spanish. Immigration as a main source of language contact sets the US apart from many other nations that, during the same period, were exporting their languages along with their cultural norms and values to other sovereign nations through invasions and colonization. Although the means of contact were different, the linguistic results were often the same: some languages fell by the wayside and died while other languages were maintained.

In Figures 2.1 and 2.2, we see the possible outcomes of contact for Indigenous languages and home languages. IndL = Indigenous languages, HmL = home language, and NL refers to the new, incoming language. In both the immigration and colonization scenarios, after a period of bilingualism, the two languages may remain as part of the community in stable bilingualism, with both languages maintained. Alternatively,

Figure 2.1 Effects of language contact on Indigenous languages.

Figure 2.2 Immigration and effects of language contact on home languages.

the Indigenous language (IndL) or home language (HmL) may succumb to pressures from the larger speech community, and speakers may shift entirely to a monolingual state and adopt the new language (NL).

The remainder of this chapter is divided into two parts. In the first Section (2.1), we introduce the relevant terminology, and then move on to examine the often complex, hierarchical relationships between speech communities in plurilingual societies, and, consequently, between languages. We will see how speech communities manage their multiple languages in stable bilingual communities, how language choice indexes self-identification and community membership, and how in multilingual societies, as in monolingual societies, language is used to unite or isolate individuals and groups through language choice. Along the way, we address related issues such as attitudes of bilinguals and monolinguals toward bilingualism, and the range of attitudes toward language mixing. In the second Section (2.2), we look at the flip side of contact—how it may first result in bilingualism but over time may also contribute to linguistic and cultural endangerment and loss. Relatedly, we will examine how nations use language to strengthen their borders and to acknowledge or suppress diversity, and what can be done to reverse endangerment.

Thinking Matters

Political Scientist Sidney Verba writes, "*Immigration has shaped the contours of this nation's history, from its founding to its present day. Immigration has shaped the nation's cities, its industries, its institutions, and laws, its literature, and its culture.*" (ocp.hul.harvard.edu/immigration.1. html). Explain what you think he means and provide some examples.

2.1 Managing Multiple Languages

2.1.1 Useful Vocabulary: A Term Is Worth a Thousand Words

To begin, let's familiarize ourselves with the relevant terminology. Though it sometimes seems like splitting hairs, the true purpose of terminology is to capture the convergence of features or characteristics which define the issues, controversies, and possibly solutions in a field of study. It's the academic equivalent of an emoji that aims to capture bundles of nuanced emotional states and meanings with single images. As a result, the boundaries between the meanings of terms are sometimes fuzzy and overlapping. Here, we present terms that have arisen from the contact of languages and cultures in plurilingual societies. Some capture the power dynamics, status, and value of languages living alongside one another in a nation, such as *majority* and *minority* languages, while others speak to the immigrant status of the speaker and the geographic and ethnic history of the language, as in the term *heritage language*.

Term	Definition and example
First language	The language a child is first exposed to and acquires naturally, without instruction, in a home environment.
Native language	The language first acquired in a home environment, but with the distinction that it also denotes an association with a nation. For example, the native language of Korea is Korean. It is often used in the context of immigration and immigrants to refer to the language of the country they moved from and that they grew up speaking before moving to another country. For example, the native language of someone from northern Vietnam now living in the US is Vietnamese.
Mother tongue	An older term that carries the same meaning as and is used interchangeably with native language.
Home language	This term, unlike the three previous, is more complex and is indexical of a number of relationships. First, 'home language' always paints a picture of a situation where there is a language used outside of the home for public activities and events—also known as the *majority language*. Therefore, the 'home language' refers to the language(s) used by a portion of the population that is considered a minority. Within a nation there may be multiple minority languages. In such cases, the term 'home language' may be used to reference any of those languages, in order to distinguish it from the majority language. Questions about home language are often seen on school forms and medical forms in order to ascertain the language needs of the student or patient. It can also be found on the US Census community survey section.

(*Continued*)

Term	Definition and example
Heritage language	Similar to home language and native language, the definition of heritage language is layered. It speaks more to the cultural connections individuals have to the language than to proficiency and use of the language per se. It is thus a combination of the concepts of minority language, home language and cultural identity, and is typically associated with the generations that follow the first generation (second, third, and so on) born after immigration to a new country and with Indigenous peoples, such as the Crow or Lakota in the US who will have different proficiency levels in and knowledge of their language due to lack of support from outside and lack of support and use from within the community. Distinguishing features of this term, then, are that heritage language speakers may or may not be frequent users of the language or particularly proficient in the language. Their connection to the language may be more through connections to family and culture than through knowledge of the language itself. Another term used interchangeably with heritage language is community language.
Minority & Majority languages	There are mixed feelings about these two terms. In many contexts and nations, 'minority' carries with it negative associations and connotations, while, in contrast, 'majority' automatically carries a positive spin. In its most neutral meaning, a minority language is a language with fewer speakers than the majority language within a community or nation. However, when it comes to languages and speakers, neutrality is not the order of the day. Whether as immigrants or descendants of immigrants, or as Indigenous groups, in many nations and communities, speakers of minority languages may, in fact, have fewer opportunities, less economic and political influence, and overall, less access to federal and community services. This unequal treatment is not about language, but language is used as one means to discriminate against and separate out communities that don't fit with the 'mainstream'. The majority language is often the national language, and the language of the political, economic, and educational systems in a nation. It is, therefore, seen as the norm.

(Continued)

Term	Definition and example
National language	Intuitively, we probably know what national language means. National language and official languages are at times used interchangeably and are, in fact, the same for many nations. It is the language that is associated with the name of the nation—for example, Swedish is the national language of Sweden, used in media and entertainment, education, politics, and all services funded at the national level. It is also the official (statutory) language. However, the designation of a national language (officially or unofficially) doesn't mean that some or all of these same services are not available in other languages, languages relevant to the immigrant and Indigenous populations. In the case of Sweden, for example, a number of languages are designated as statutory provincial languages, which according to Ethnologue means that the "language is used in education, work, mass media, and government within major administrative subdivisions of a nation".
Official language	We often see this term used by linguists and non-linguists. Official language, also called **statutory language**, makes a legal statement about the status of a language in a nation. The term is sometimes used along with 'national language', although as mentioned previously, a national language is not necessarily the official language. Official means statutory, governed by national law. And for some nations, for example, Canada, India, and Switzerland, the status of official and national languages are stated in their national statutory provisions. For instance, the Canadian Official Language Rights Act affirms English and French as the official languages of Canada, and further explains what that means: The purpose of the *Official Languages Rights Act* is to:

- ensure respect for English and French and ensure equality of status and equal rights and privileges as to their use in federal institutions;
- support the development of English and French linguistic minority communities; and
- advance the equal status and use of English and French.

In other passages, the Act also supports the rights of employees to use the official language of their choice (either French or English) in the workplace. (www.officialla nguages.gc.ca/en/language_rights/act)

(*Continued*)

Term	Definition and example
	A case where the national language is not an official language is that of the US. Though English is the national language it is not the *official* national language. It is by virtue of its widespread use across the nation and in official and non-official capacities and contexts, such as health and educational services, that it is *de facto* the national language. It should be noted that in the case of the US, 32 states have declared English as their official language. Alaska has recognized 20 Indigenous languages alongside English as official, and Hawaii has included Hawaiian as official.
De facto	The term *de facto* is Latin and literally means 'of fact'. In the context of our discussions, when used with bilingualism, as in a *de facto* bilingual/plurilingual nation, it means that, although not declared by law (*de jure*), the nation is in fact bilingual by practice. In other words, more than one language is in widespread use. It does not mean that all or even the majority of citizens are bilingual, nor does it claim that the country is under any obligation to guarantee or encourage services or education in more than one language (the national language). The US is a good example of a *de facto* plurilingual nation.
De jure	As mentioned above, *de jure*, also Latin, means 'by law', and affects the entire nation or state. *De jure* or official/statutory languages are often written into a country's or state's constitution. See the explanation of official language, previous.
Lingua franca	A lingua franca is any language in wide use, nationally and/or internationally, used to bridge the language gap among speakers from different language backgrounds. The language(s) that take on such a role are associated with power and prestige. Which languages serve as a lingua franca may change over time. Historically, they would have been the language of literature, poetry, law, diplomacy, and commerce. Greek, Latin, French, Italian, Arabic, and Persian have all served as lingua francas at some point in history. Today, English is considered the leading lingua franca globally. The influence of English is so great that even in non-English-speaking countries, English can be seen in advertisements solely intended for internal consumption. We will discuss this aspect of English in more depth later in this chapter.
Diglossia	Generally speaking, a speech community in which two languages or two varieties of a language are used in different domains for different social and communicative functions has been called a diglossic community. In Section 2.1.2 we take a closer look at the concept of diglossia and some communities that have been labeled as diglossic.

(Continued)

Term	Definition and example
Primary language & Secondary language	Not to be mistaken with the term primary bilingualism, which describes the methods by which a speaker becomes bilingual, a primary language is the language that a speaker uses most often and in more contexts. It frequently is or becomes the speaker's dominant language. It follows, then, that a speaker's secondary language is one that is used less often by the speaker and/or the speech community to which the speaker belongs. The primary-secondary nature of the relationship between the two languages is labyrinthine, in part dependent on domains of use of each language, in part conditional on the value of each language in a larger national and/or global context, and in part because of the many other language-specific factors discussed in Chapter 1.
Dominant language	A bilingual speaker's dominant language is the one he or she is most proficient in and may be the one used most often by the speaker. Or it may correspond to the speaker's first/home language, especially when the speaker has learned his or her other languages in adulthood, even if it's not the language used most often. In the context of a community or nation, dominant language refers to the language used publicly, and may be the de jure or de facto official language.
Community of practice	Most of us belong to more than one community of practice. This term is used to describe groups who share linguistic and cultural norms and expectations and are often bound together through language(s) and language use. One community of practice bilinguals typically belong to is the one defined by their bilingualism and biculturalism—they are bound, then, specifically by the cultural norms and practices that come with each of their languages. It is often the case that all members of bilingual communities of practice don't share the same degree of language proficiency in or comfort using their languages. Nevertheless, they feel connected through shared cultural values, norms, and other social practices involving the knowledge, use, and interpretations of language. Bilinguals may also be members of each of their individual languages' monolingual communities of practice, depending on their communicative abilities and comfort in each of the languages. Thus, an Arabic-English bilingual in England can be a part of the monolingual English-speaking community, the monolingual Arabic-speaking community, and the bilingual Arabic-English community of practice.

2.1.2 Stable Bilingualism +/- Diglossia

As illustrated in Figure 2.3, stable bilingualism can lead to a diglossic bilingual community or a community of bilinguals without diglossia.

Diglossic bilingualism: The term diglossia was first used in 1959 by Charles Ferguson to describe four speech communities in which all or most members are bilingual in two varieties of the same language. Ferguson concluded that each of the two varieties in each community, for example Swiss German and Standard German in Switzerland, has its own distinct social domains in which it is *expected* to be used. One variety is considered more formal and used in professional settings, while the other is deemed to be more casual, used with family and friends and other informal contexts. Note that in a diglossic community, most members have to use both varieties. Over time, the concept of diglossia has been extended to bilingualism to describe the relationship of coexisting languages to each other. In diglossic bilingualism, each language has its own social circle and functions (or domains of use). Diglossic communities can be found throughout the world, but are more commonly an outcome of colonization or present in border communities and less so a result of immigration. The new language, brought in by colonizers, drapes over the existing national language but does not replace it. Sometimes the domains intersect, but mostly they are kept distinct and separate. The usual division of function is between the informal language of daily life, family and relationships, and the formal/institutional language of education and government services. Both languages may or may not be official. It is possible for a speech community to have more than two languages as part of this division, in other words, to be tri- or quatro-glossic. The main point of interest in any such communities is the fact that every language in the mix has a function and domain of use and is, therefore, valued and maintained. To be valued does not mean, however, that each language

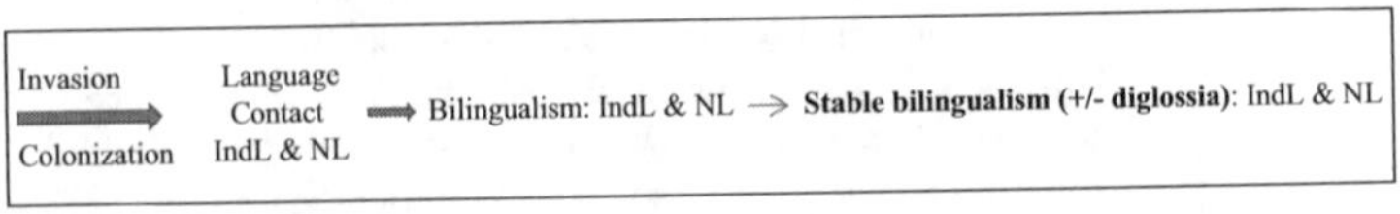

Invasion / Colonization Language Contact IndL & NL ⟹ Bilingualism: IndL & NL → **Stable bilingualism (+/- diglossia)**: IndL & NL

Figure 2.3 Creation of bilingual communities with and without diglossia.

has the same status in the speech community. Typically, the new language takes on more prestigious and official status, especially in the domains of government functions and services and of education. The Indigenous language remains a crucially important part of the fabric of society and of connection to the cultural heritage of the speakers, and continues as the language of everyday life, local services, shops, home, religion, and relationships. Morocco is often cited as a clear example of a di-/multi-glossic nation. As a result of several invasions and other forms of contact over a number of centuries, Morocco is a multilingual nation housing several languages, as shown in this brief history of contact and the various languages and their roles in Morocco:

- **Standard Arabic**—Official (constitutional/de jure) national language.
  Arabic was brought in with Islam in the 8th century and has remained an important part of the cultural, religious, and educational lives of Moroccans. It is used for all documents written in Arabic. Because Standard Arabic is the language that ushered in Islam, the main religion in Morocco, it is associated most obviously with religious practices but also with traditional, socially conservative attitudes in general. Because Standard Arabic is a formal and mostly written language, its use is directly tied to literacy.
- **Moroccan Arabic**—De facto national working language, widely used in everyday interactions and informal contexts. It is a spoken language, with Standard Arabic as its written counterpart. Because it is a spoken language, Moroccan Arabic has nearly twice as many users as Standard Arabic.
- **Tamazight**, also known as Berber—Official (constitutional/de jure since 2011), a language indigenous to Morocco and Northern Africa that has recently been recognized as an official language.
- **Spanish**—A shifting language (see language shift later in this section), with fewer families passing the language to their children. Spanish has lost its usefulness and status to French and English, two Western languages which are either nationally or internationally more relevant to Moroccans.
- **French**—De facto national working language, used institutionally across the country, beyond the home and community. It is

the language of administration, commerce, education, and industry. The colonization of Morocco by France, although relatively short-lived (1912–1956), had a profound effect on the country and Moroccan culture. Morocco regained its independence in 1956, but French has remained an important part of Moroccan culture and identity. It is generally considered the language of science, technology, administration, and art. Because of its history in Morocco, French is considered the language of the educated and the powerful elite. It is further associated with modernity and serves as a link and conduit to the West. Children most often learn French in primary school, or even younger in preschool. Given these attitudes toward French, it is no wonder Moroccan-French diglossia continues to be robust.

- **English**—Although a relative newcomer to the language scene in Morocco, English has become an important language on a par with French with respect to its status among other languages. Like French, it is associated with power, prestige, and education. It represents modernity and is an important link to Western ideology and culture. English, through association with American culture, has an additional pop culture, "cool" dimension which French lacks. Consequently, English has become the language of choice as a second language to acquire through schooling or at least in school.

Bilingualism without diglossia: Can there be societal bilingualism/multilingualism without diglossia? In other words, can multiple languages coexist in a nation without the majority of the population knowing and using the languages in different domains as described previously? Let's begin with a qualified "yes". Bilingualism without national-level diglossia is commonly the result of immigration. By this we mean that incoming immigrants, out of desire and necessity, become bilinguals, but the host nation's language practices do not change; the immigrant population is expected to learn the host nation's language, but not vice versa. Consequently, the scope of the immigrants' home language use becomes restricted to the home and possibly to a small neighborhood of other immigrants from the same linguistic background. Over time, the neighborhood may expand to include family-run shops and restaurants where the home language can be used. Consequently, immigrants become bilingual as they acquire the national language of their host country. For new arrivals and at least the first generation after them, diglossia becomes part of their everyday lives, as they choose from their two languages which to use in various domains, including when to use a mix of the two (codeswitching). An obvious divide between the languages would be to use the heritage language at home and with other members of the same bilingual communities, and, of course, with monolinguals of the heritage language. The national language is then reserved for most other public functions such as work, school, shopping, medical services, etc. This state of heritage language/host language diglossia can be maintained by individuals for generations as long as the home language and culture are valued and receive positive recognition at the community level, locally, and beyond, even when societal diglossia is not supported.

Language shift: However, because immigrant populations rarely have any political or social power in the host country, at least not for the first few generations, their language is not deemed necessary or useful for the host country, and, therefore, is not actively supported. Consequently, in many cases, a diglossic relationship between the heritage language (home language) and the national language (host language), where the immigrant community maintains the heritage language across generations, is short-lived and gives way to *language shift*. As the term suggests, a linguistic conversion takes place; the host language gradually replaces the home language and the diglossic community becomes a monolingual community of host-language speakers.

Of course, individual diglossia can and does continue. This means that at least some members of immigrant speech communities maintain the home language and culture and pass it on to their children along with the host country's language, cultural norms, and expectations. Figure 2.4 reviews the linguistic outcomes of immigration. HmL = home/heritage language (the language brought in with immigrants). HL = host nation's language. Language contact borne out of immigration initially mostly results in bilingual immigrants, though some of the older immigrants

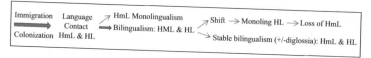

Figure 2.4 Immigration's effects on home language.

may remain monolingual in their home language. Further down the line, Home-Language-Host Language bilingualism can maintain across generations, or a shift to monolingual host language may occur.

Thinking Matters

Table 2.1 shows 5-year estimates by the US Census Bureau of 10 of the 38 top languages spoken at home and the respondents' English-speaking abilities. You can find the full table at https://factfinder.census.gov/faces/tableservices/jsf/pages/productview.xhtml?src=CF, where you can compare the total number of speakers for each language in the earliest version of the report with the numbers in the latest version. For example, the total number of Greek speakers was 331,665 in 2009. The number dropped to 282,863 in 2017. Which language groups' numbers have stayed steady, which have grown, and which have decreased? What do you think accounts for the changes or lack of changes in these numbers?

2.2 Maintaining Bilingualism

A factor that bears considerably on whether one becomes bilingual and whether bilingualism is maintained and passed on to subsequent generations is the real and perceived usefulness of each of the language(s)—whether the language is valued within and outside of the speaker's community. Take for example the use of English in non-English-speaking countries. A 2014 survey requested by the European Commission shows English to be the most popular other language among EU bilinguals, with 38% of European respondents reporting English as one of their languages, a far larger percentage than the next four popular second languages spoken in Europe: French at 12%, German at 11%, Spanish at 7%, and Russian at 5%.

Thinking Matters

Why do you think English is so popular in non-English-speaking countries?

Table 2.1 Partial table of language spoken at home by ability to speak English for the population 5 years and over. American Community Survey 5 year estimates, 2013–2017

	United States	
	Estimate	Margin of error
Total:	301,150,892	+/−3,777
Speak only English	236,929,699	+/−184,625
Spanish:	39,769,281	+/−111,096
Speak English "very well"	23,411,399	+/−61,637
Speak English less than "very well"	16,357,882	+/−60,449
French (incl. Cajun):	1,203,941	+/−9,736
Speak English "very well"	958,091	+/−8,288
Speak English less than "very well"	245,850	+/−4,366
Haitian:	824,884	+/−14,377
Speak English "very well"	489,302	+/−9,746
Speak English less than "very well"	335,582	+/−7,166
Italian:	610,253	+/−7,181
Speak English "very well"	446,413	+/−6,143
Speak English less than "very well"	163,840	+/−3,283
Portuguese:	720,092	+/−9,218
Speak English "very well"	461,090	+/−7,597
Speak English less than "very well"	259,002	+/−5,080
German:	936,083	+/−8,497
Speak English "very well"	794,611	+/−7,168
Speak English less than "very well"	141,472	+/−3,242
Yiddish, Pennsylvania Dutch or other West Germanic languages:	484,057	+/−6,758
Speak English "very well"	343,935	+/−6,060
Speak English less than "very well"	140,122	+/−3,078
Greek:	282,863	+/−4,955
Speak English "very well"	210,378	+/−4,143
Speak English less than "very well"	72,485	+/−2,446
Russian:	907,362	+/−9,812
Speak English "very well"	505,575	+/−6,176
Speak English less than "very well"	401,787	+/−6,352
Polish:	534,704	+/−6,892
Speak English "very well"	326,993	+/−5,108
Speak English less than "very well"	207,711	+/−3,747

(Source: https://factfinder.census.gov/faces/tableservices/jsf/pages/product view.xhtml?pid=ACS_17_5YR_B16001&prodType=table)

The high percentage for English in the Commission's report is attributed to the dominance of English in business, which has stayed stable since the 2005 survey. In 2012, the Harvard Business Review reported,

> English is now the global language of business. More and more multinational companies are mandating English as the common corporate language—Airbus, Daimler-Chrysler, Fast Retailing, Nokia, Renault, Samsung, SAP, Technicolor, and Microsoft in Beijing, to name a few—in an attempt to facilitate communication and performance across geographically diverse functions and business endeavors.

Similarly, a poll conducted for Reuters by Ipsos Global Public Affairs found that 61% of the 16,344 adult employees in 23 non-English-speaking countries used English more often than any other language when conducting business outside of their own countries.

Another reason for the popularity of English can be attributed to the global influence of American pop culture. Whether the contact is on-site or virtual, as in the case of the influence of American pop culture, knowing and using English has coolness attached to it. The photograph in Figure 2.5 shows a shop window in Tehran, Iran. The phrase "Happy Mother's Day" and "Spring Collection" are in English as part of their "Mother's Day" sale on headscarves. Scarves are an essential part of the hijab dress code, a custom completely antithetical to Western "cool". Nevertheless, given the complicated private and public persona that Iranian women navigate, the use of English

Figure 2.5 Shop window, Tehran, Iran, 2014.

Figure 2.6 English and Russian sign outside a shop in Tbilisi, Georgia.
(Source: MicheleB, Shutterstock)

connects the product, the shop, its owner, and those who shop there to a more modern, Western world. Likewise, in Figure 2.6 we see a sign in Russian and English advertising the shop's wine ice cream in Tbilisi, Georgia. Although the national statutory language of Georgia is Georgian, the sign is in Russian—the de facto national working language—and in English. In Chapter 3, we will further investigate the use of multiple languages in public venues and discuss what the incorporation of multiple languages may signal.

By the same token, maintenance of the home language in immigrant contexts relies heavily on a recognized need beyond the heritage and cultural connection. Both those who will be passing the home language on to the next generation and the generation receiving it must perceive the home language as essential to their lives. For this reason, community support, official state support, and large numbers of speakers are essential to the maintenance of the home language beyond the second/third generations. Community support includes the availability of media and cultural functions such as religious services in the home language. Official state support can mean anything from use of the home language regularly for at least some official/governmental services to funding bilingual education. Official school use of heritage languages also signals respect for the language and culture and brings with it recognition by the majority language users. In Section 2.4, "Language Endangerment", we discuss language maintenance at more length.

2.3 Attitudes Toward Bilingualism

More than a half-century ago, in a book entitled *Language Loyalty in the United States*, Fishman et al. noted that

> many Americans have long been of the opinion that bilingualism is 'a good thing' if it was acquired via travel (preferably to Paris) or via formal education (preferably at Harvard) but that it is a 'bad thing' if it was acquired from one's immigrant parents or grandparents.
>
> (1966, pp. 122–123)

Thinking Matters

Before moving forward, take a moment to think about and discuss Fishman et al.'s quote. To what extent do you think this statement is true today?

The language(s) and/or *variety*(ies) speakers use have long been exploited to judge and to justify subjective attitudes and behaviors toward subsets of society. Before we begin our discussion of attitudes toward bilingualism, a few general points about languages and their varieties:

(1) Every language has a number of *varieties*, also known as *dialects*, associated with it. For example, 'English' can be British, American, Australian, Indian, or many of the other national varieties of English spoken in the world.

(2) Each national variety has a number of its own varieties distinguished by region (for example, some American English varieties include Kentuckian, North Texan, East Ender Bostonian, Southern California Valley), by ethnicity/race (for example, African-American Vernacular English [AAVE]), and by social factors such as age, gender, and socioeconomic class. Each national variety has an overall standard form associated with it, the form that is taught in schools, and heard on national TV and radio newscasts, for example. But there are also regional standard forms as well.

These varieties are a mix of the national standard plus regional accents and vocabulary.

(3) National standard varieties are used in schools and other educational contexts as well as in national/state level addresses by public officials, and in speech by some radio and television newscasters. The variety that becomes the national standard is a reflection of which group of citizens, which *community of speakers*, is in power at any given time.

Adger and Christian (2006) provide an apt summary of the status of "standard" and "non-standard" varieties:

> dialect prejudice is endemic in public life, widely tolerated, and institutionalized in social enterprises that affect almost everyone, such as education and the media. There is limited knowledge about and little regard for [by the general public] linguistic study showing that all varieties of a language display systematicity and that the elevated social position of standard varieties has no scientific linguistic basis.

(p. 2546)

Essentially, when we judge a language or a dialect as 'bad' or ungrammatical, or not as good as another language, we are frequently judging the speakers themselves. After all, languages and dialects are all equally systematic and rule-governed: there are no ungrammatical or primitive or bad languages or dialects. Sure, we've been told by parents, teachers, even people we hardly know, not to use *ain't* (and my spell check just tried to "correct" this word!) or double negatives. Some of these same people, however, enjoy and sing along with performers such as Elvis Presley ("You Ain't Nothing But a Hound Dog"), the Rolling Stones ("I Can't Get No Satisfaction"), Pink Floyd ("We Don't Need No Education'), Marvin Gaye ("Ain't Nothing Like the Real Thing"), and countless country and rap singers and songs, which all contain the scorned double negative. This seeming contradiction reveals what Fishman et al. noted in the quote above: that it's not so much the language but who's using it and for what purpose on which our judgments are based.

Attitudes toward bilingualism are nearly inseparable from attitudes toward immigration, from both the host nation and the immigrant population. Unfortunately, language, as one of our most salient characteristics as humans, has often been caught in the crossfire and used to identify and discriminate against various nationalities and racial/ethnic groups. Positive and negative feelings about language are nearly always about the speaker and the speech community they belong to, not about the language itself. Rooted in long-held stereotypes and biases that are based on ethnicity, race, gender, class, age, religion, and even what region or country the speakers are from (rural, urban, north, south, Middle Eastern, etc.), comments about certain dialects sounding uneducated or some languages sounding harsh or unkind often reveal a hostile attitude toward the speakers of the dialect or language (see Table 2.2).

In a groundbreaking Canadian study, Lambert, Hodgson, Gardner, and Fillenbaum (1960) used an experimental technique called a *matched-guise test* to examine language as a feature of national or cultural identity, and the associated attitudes toward the identities as propagated through stereotypes. Listening to recorded passages in French and in English, monolingual French- and monolingual English-speaking Canadian university students in Montreal were asked to rate the desirability of the tape-recorded speakers, including their intelligence, dependability, ability to achieve success, etc. The participants believed they were listening to monolingual English speakers and monolingual French speakers when in fact they were listening to the same bilingual French-English individuals who had recorded the same passages in the two different languages. Lambert et al. had hypothesized that English-speaking students would rate the English speakers more favorably, and French students would favor the French speakers. To their surprise, only half of their prediction was borne out: The English students did in fact rate the English speakers in the passages more favorably (more intelligent, dependable, likely to succeed, etc.), but so did the French students. Lambert et al. interpreted the latter findings (French students favoring the English speakers on tape) to be influenced by the generally higher socioeconomic status of English speakers and the resulting pervasive negative stereotypes attached to French speakers in Montreal at that time. The matched-guise technique has been used widely and has proven to be a useful instrument to access language attitudes in multilingual/multi-dialectal contexts. The following is an example from Kaplan-Weinger:

Table 2.2 Example of Matched-Guise continua

X -- X	
happy	sad
X -- X	
polite	rude
X -- X	
dishonest	truthful

It [the matched-guise test] works this way: A speaker who is bilingual or multilingual is recorded reading aloud a given passage in each of her languages. Each of the different languages is a guise, or disguise, for the same speaker. A Portuguese, French, Spanish, and English multilingual may read aloud, for example, a short children's story in each of the languages in which she is proficient. The recordings are played to subjects whose task is to rate each speaker on a set of semantic differential scales. Each scale is a continuum with one of a pair of adjectives that are antonyms at each end. After listening to the first speaker, the subject indicates on a continuum her feelings about the speaker.

(Mahootian, Kaplan-Weiner, Gebhardt, & Hallett, 2017, p. 254)

Attitudes toward bilinguals and bilingualism naturally differ across speech communities, nations, and generations. In the US, as in a number of other countries, immigration continues to be a hot-button issue. Despite America's rich history and repute as a land built by immigrants, within a century of the initial settlers, anti-immigrant sentiments were already brewing. By the mid-1700s, it is estimated that half the population of what is now the US was bilingual, with a third being German speakers from Germany. Notwithstanding this fact, as more and more immigrants, mostly from Western Europe, found their way to the New World, language-focused rumblings were emerging, all of which proved to be anti-immigration stances at their core. The old concerns over immigration, like the current concerns, were really about keeping "others" out because they were different and could change the status quo. At the center of the attitudes, in many cases, differences in language were used to demonize newcomers.[1] Various prominent figures railed against German and Germans; later, others decried immigration by the Irish, the Italians, the Jews, the Poles, the Mexicans, and other Latinx, and the list goes on. By 1910, roughly 11% of the 92 million members of the population spoke a language other than English at home. Although this was a smaller percentage than in the decades past, as the country grew, so did mistaken concerns of the effects of immigration on the economy, safety, and, bizarrely, the effects of their bilingualism on intelligence! Rumbaut and Massey (2013, p. 1) write:

> Much of this early social-scientific work was conducted in America, at a time of great concern with the flood of immigrants from Europe (roughly, 1900–1920). The intelligence tests of the time were very culture-specific, and non-white, non-English-speaking, non-northern-European, non-educated individuals fared poorly. In this unenlightened climate, measured intelligence was seen to correlate strongly with competence in English, and Florence Goodenough–an important educational psychologist who worked with Lewis Terman, the developer of the Stanford–Binet intelligence test–actually wrote that 'the use of a foreign language in the home is one of the chief factors in producing mental retardation'.
>
> (1926, p. 393)

By the 1940s, immigrant families believed that they needed to raise their children as monolingual English speakers in order to give them the greatest opportunities for success in America. Consequently, many children born into immigrant families in the 1940s, 1950s, and 1960s grew up speaking only one language, English, because parents discouraged their children from using the heritage language. This sentiment has changed somewhat over the last four-and-a-half decades as public awareness of the benefits of bilingualism and federal support for bilingual education has increased.

Although we started with a quote about bilingualism in America, that does not mean that the same attitudes are not found elsewhere. All around the globe, language is equated with national identity and, therefore, to great extent, with personal identity. Most people associate languages with nations and their citizens. In France, the French speak French. In Japan, the Japanese speak Japanese. In Bulgaria, Bulgarians speak Bulgarian, and so on. Consequently, if you have grown up speaking another language in addition to the national language, or if you speak the national language with an accent, you may be regarded as someone who doesn't belong to the dominant group. So what happens if you are a bilingual living in Japan and the native language of the community with which you closely identify and which has existed there for over 1,200 years is not Japanese, but is Ainu? Or you are one of 130,000 Corsican-French speakers in France? Or you are an ethnic Kurd living in Turkey and bilingual in Kurdish and Turkish? In each of these cases, the Indigenous, non-dominant languages have had to struggle for their existence. In all multilingual cases, if the language has official/statutory status, is acknowledged as a/the de facto national language, or at the least receives institutional funding and educational support, the members of the related communities of practice (i.e., the bilinguals) will receive various degrees of acknowledgment and respect. And depending on the level of acknowledgment within the communities, members are more likely to pass the home language along to their children and to uphold related cultural traditions.

Conversely, if the community is not welcomed or respected by the dominant ethno-linguistic group, the language, as a representative of the speakers, also elicits negative responses. A case in point is the plight of Latinx of Mexican origin in the US, as they navigate their linguistic and ethnic heritage and identity. Despite the fact that Spanish is a language that has long been part of high school, college, and university offerings, Mexican and Dominican Spanish have had low social value and negative associations. Consequently, Latinx immigrants struggle with maintaining their language and heritage. In their study of language and ethnic identity in the US, Bourhis and Marshall (1999) write that although Spanish speakers constitute the largest linguistic minority in the US,

> Spanish speakers are caught in a dilemma: To appear to be 'good Americans', they feel pressured to shift to English as quickly as possible; but they also recognize that in the long run this shift may be achieved at the cost of losing their mother tongue and their Hispanic cultural and ethnic identity.

(p. 250)

This "dilemma" is aptly voiced in the 1997 film *Selena*, when Selena says, "We have to be more Mexican than the Mexicans and more American than the Americans, both at the same time. It's exhausting!" (www.youtube.com/watch?v=Sw5bA8cVF-E)

At the same time that Spanish speakers are made to feel unwelcome, Spanish has been a staple in US high school and college foreign language choices. Furthermore, we have a federal holiday named after the explorer who opened the door to Spain and Spanish in the Americas. So clearly, it's not Spanish that's at issue but where the speakers are from that matters. At the end of the day, it is not difficult to understand that whatever attitudes and biases toward bilingualism spring forth, they simply boil down to prejudices held against the members of the related speech community, often a minority of Indigenous peoples or immigrants. So, then, how can multiple languages survive in plurilingual societies? The fact is that they don't all survive. For example, for most of us living in the US, English is not our heritage language. We hail from many and varied ancestries—Italian, Irish, Swedish, Chinese, Greek, Korean, Polish, Persian, Vietnamese, Cherokee, Tagalog, Blackfoot, and another 400 or so other languages and cultures. However, given that the majority of Americans are monolingual, it's obvious that many families and individuals have not maintained or passed along their heritage languages. In the next section, we will learn why some plurilingual communities have been able to maintain their languages while other communities have not.

Take a moment to think about the neighborhood, community, and country in which you live and answer the following questions:

- Are there multiple coexisting languages/dialects in any of these settings?
- Are there community members who speak more than one of the languages/dialects?
- Are there places in the community where one language is required or preferred?

2.4 Language Endangerment and Revitalization

As mentioned earlier, contact may first result in stable bilingualism, but over time may also contribute to linguistic and cultural endangerment and loss, and overall, loss of diversity nationally and globally. How does contact contribute to language endangerment? We'll start again with a few key concepts and terms. First, what does it mean when a language is *endangered*? As the word implies, it means that the language is in danger of dying, of becoming extinct. *Language death*

Figure 2.7 Language awareness sign along Interstate 90 within the Crow Reservation in south-central Montana.

(Source: Courtesy of Lewis Gebhardt, 2016)

occurs when there are no longer any speakers of a language left to pass it on to others. *Language extinction* occurs when there is no record of the language left behind to revive and revitalize the language. Many *Indigenous languages* in various parts of the world have suffered this fate, with many more in danger of the same outcome. A language is said to be indigenous to a region when it has been spoken in an area for many generations AND has historical and cultural roots in the region. The United Nations provides a more detailed, legal definition:

> Indigenous communities, peoples and nations are those which, having a historical continuity with pre-invasion and pre-colonial societies that developed on their territories, consider themselves distinct from other sectors of the societies now prevailing on those territories, or parts of them.
>
> (www.un.org/development/desa/ indigenouspeoples/about-us.html)

Examples of Indigenous communities of practice include the Ainu of Japan, Sammi speakers in Norway, speakers of Native American[2] languages of North America, some rooted in the history of a region where the language developed. For example, Crow, Navajo, Cherokee, Blackfoot, Cree, Inuit, Ojibway, Dakota are Indigenous to North America (what is now the USA and Canada). Gebhardt writes:

> For a language to survive, to be passed on to succeeding generations, it must be perceived as useful for speakers. ... indigenous languages are falling behind. It's thought that about half the world's languages have fewer than 10,000 speakers and that perhaps a quarter of the world's languages have fewer than 1,000 speakers ... . [I]t's likely that hundreds of the world's languages will die in the coming decades.
>
> (Mahootian et al., 2017, p. 180)

Thinking Matters

Take a close look at the photograph in Figure 2.7. What does it tell you about the status of the Indigenous language, Crow, a Siouan language spoken on the Crow reservation in southern Montana?

The shift from home language to the new language is a process that typically takes three or more generations, depending on the cause of the contact. There are many examples of war-induced or other threatening forms of contact whereby the home language is outlawed or consistently denigrated and consequently lost within a few generations. As a result, only older community members know and use the language regularly. In these cases, especially with languages like Native American languages for which there were little or no written documentation, the language dies. At the time Europeans descended upon the Americas, it is estimated that there were approximately 300 Native American languages spoken in what is now the US and Canada, and more than 2,000, including Indigenous languages of Central and South America. Of the 300, it is estimated that nearly half have become extinct. Of the remaining 150 or so languages, more than half have fewer than

Table 2.3 Sample Native North American languages spoken in the United States

	No. of speakers	Speaks English less than "very well"
Navajo	**166,826**	**35,250**
Other Native North American languages	**197,505**	**29,548**
Aleut	995	170
Pacific Gulf Yupik	70	—
Eskimo	1,270	265
Inupik	6,740	1,365
St. Lawrence Island Yupik	1,070	285
Yupik	19,750	5,930
Algonquian	1,030	265
Arapaho	1,065	50
Atsina	55	—
Blackfoot	1,450	65
Cheyenne	1,920	175
Cree	870	190

(Source: Adapted from US Census Bureau, 2009–2013 American Community Survey. www.census.gov/data/tables/2013/demo/2009-2013-lang-tables.html)

1,000 speakers, and several have fewer than 10. Navajo is the most robust, with 166,000 speakers. Table 2.3 presents a sample of some of the Native North American languages spoken in the US. For the full list of 152 languages, visit US Census Bureau, 2009–2013 American Community Survey (https://www.census.gov/data/tables/2013/demo/2009-2013-lang-tables.html).

The history of the birth of what is now the US is one that includes eradication of many Indigenous peoples and languages, and the outlawing of their languages and cultures during the height of settlement and westward expansion. The clearest (and most shocking) examples are from language policies aimed at Native Americans. In a heritage language report for the Center for Applied Linguistics[3], Warhol reports (2011),

Historically, the federal government employed schooling as the primary tool for cultural and linguistic eradication to assimilate

Native American communities ... . Therefore, despite policies that now protect and preserve Native American languages, 90% of Native American languages are moribund or endangered (Moseley, 2010). ... The sole goal of education was to civilize the American Indian, thus creating a homogeneous American population with little linguistic or cultural difference. As early as 1819, the government had passed the Civilization Act, which provided funding for missionaries and others "for introducing among them (American Indians) the habits and arts of civilization" (Reyhner & Eder, 2004, p. 43), including a mandatory English language policy. This was especially prominent during the mandatory boarding school period from 1879 to 1934. Government boarding schools were able to isolate Indian children from their families and communities and implement an extreme deculturation experience (Tiersma, 2010). Children were regularly rounded up and forced from their homes to attend these schools. Punishment for speaking their Native languages was common and frequent (Adams, 1995). Between 1879 and 1905, 25 off-reservation boarding schools were established and by 1930, 136 on- and off- reservation boarding schools existed serving 32,316 Native children (Reyhner & Eder, 2004).

(Adapted from www.cal.org/heritage/
pdfs/briefs/native-american-language-
policy.pdf, pp. 1–2)

Thinking Matters

It is estimated that there are between 10,000 and 22,000 speakers of Cherokee. Yet Cherokee is considered an endangered language. Go to the following sites to read and watch short videos about the Cherokee: www.mustgo.com/worldlanguages/cherokee/ and www.youtube.com/watch?v=B5Prv_E0M78. After watching both video clips, answer the following questions: Why is Cherokee considered endangered? How many native speakers of Cherokee remain today? How did Cherokee become endangered? What is the link between language and culture?

2.4.1 Protecting, Revitalizing, and Maintaining Indigenous Languages

Although it seems like an impossible task, some nearly extinct or dormant languages have been revitalized. The task of doing so is multipronged and requires community commitment at local and national levels. The language must be made visible and its usefulness demonstrated through institutional support, such as by funding the language as part of a K–12 curriculum, producing media in the language, or funding cultural events. Most importantly, the community itself must have a central role in the process, as in the case of Crow. Efforts to revitalize Crow have picked up steam in the last decade as more native Crow speakers have gotten involved with revitalization programs that include the development of language materials for the teaching of Crow to primary students, and undergoing training to teach Crow. International organizations such as UNESCO have, as part of their mission, the protection of languages and cultures, as stated here:

> Languages, with their complex implications for identity, communication, social integration, education and development, are of strategic importance for people and the planet. There is growing awareness that languages play a vital role in development, not only in ensuring cultural diversity and intercultural dialogue, but also in attaining quality education for all and strengthening cooperation, in building inclusive knowledge societies and preserving cultural heritage, and in mobilizing political will for applying the benefits of science and technology to sustainable development. UNESCO is thus taking urgent action to encourage broad and international commitment to promoting multilingualism and linguistic diversity, including the safeguarding of endangered languages.
>
> (www.unesco.org/new/en/culture/themes/
> endangered-languages/biodiversity-and-
> linguistic-diversity/)

In 2003, UNESCO's Ad Hoc Group on Endangered Languages produced a document identifying and describing nine factors that, taken together, help determine the level of vitality and/or endangerment of a language. In order of importance, these factors are:

(1) Intergenerational language transmission;
(2) Absolute number of speakers;
(3) Proportion of speakers within the total population;
(4) Shifts in domains of language use;
(5) Response to new domains and media;
(6) Materials for language education and literacy;
(7) Governmental and institutional language attitudes and policies, including official status and use;
(8) Community members' attitudes toward their own language; and
(9) Type and quality of documentation.

                    (www.unesco.org/new/fileadmin/MULTIMEDIA
                              /HQ/CLT/pdf/Language_vitality_and_
                                          endangerment_EN.pdf)

Although intergenerational transmission is paramount in the survival and revitalization of a language, taken alone it's not always sufficient to maintain a minority language. Nor is factor 2; even when the language has a large number of speakers, that does not guarantee survival of the minority language. As discussed earlier, support from institutions outside of the immediate language community, especially state and federal recognition and funding, are essential to the survival of Indigenous languages. It has also been shown that the survival potential of a threatened language is significantly increased where there is a positive attitude towards the language from within the community of users and from the majority language community. The ninth factor, language documentation, is where linguists and community members together have the most responsibility. The most useful documents for language preservation and revitalization are written texts based on audio- and video-taped natural speech and interviews with native speakers, transcribed, and translated. It bears repeating that none of these factors are sufficient, independently, to determine the future of an Indigenous/non-dominant language. Rather, a combination of the factors will render a more accurate determination. For a firsthand report of young American Indians and how they identify, read Amanda Blackhorse's 2015 article *Do You Prefer 'Native American' or 'American Indian' (Indian Country Today*, https://newsmaven.io/indiancountrytoday/archive/blackhorse-do-you-prefer-native-american-or-american-indian-kHWRPJqIGU6X3FTVdMi9EQ/).

2.5 Summary

In this chapter, we've looked at societal bilingualism, how it manifests, and how it may be maintained or lost. Relatedly, we've discussed attitudes toward bilingualism and management of multiple languages by bilingual and by diglossic communities. We've learned about the effects of language contact on non-dominant languages, from endangerment to death, and the steps needed for revitalization. Moreover, we've seen that language, whether at a community or an individual level, is a resource. The language variety speakers choose in which to communicate can signal solidarity, exclusion, and intimacy. It can be used to pull rank and reinforce a speaker's status. In Chapter 3, we take a closer look at the how and the why of language mixing and of language choice.

Discussion Questions and Projects

1. In his book *Bilingual: Life and Reality*, François Grosjean says, "In the end, the more monolingual a group or country is, the more difficult it is for the society to understand that bilinguals are a real asset to a nation in terms of what they can bring to cross-cultural communication and understanding" (2010, p. 107). Do you agree or disagree with this statement? Explain your answer.

2. Using the US English website, http://us-english.org/view/8, find answers to the following questions:
   (a) Look up the state in which you live or are attending college. What is the policy on English as the official language of that state and of the US?
   (b) How many official languages are there in the US?
   (c) In which US states is English the official language?
   (d) In which countries is English (one of) the official languages(s)?

3. Go to https://www.census.gov/data/tables/2013/demo/2009-2013-lang-tables.html and click on Detailed Languages Spoken at Home and Ability to Speak English for the Population 5 Years and Over for United States: 2009–2013 link to download a detailed table of the 350 languages spoken in the home by US residents. Based on the numbers, what are the top ten non-English home languages in the US? Pick one of the languages you are least familiar with to

research and write a report. Find out what has brought speakers of this language to the US.

4. How many official languages are there in India? How many national languages? What are the top three languages spoken in India and how many people speak each?

5. What are the top five endangered languages in the world? How many of these five are Indigenous to the USA?

6. Go to the most recent US Census site and select the American Community Survey. What terminology is used to ask about languages and language use? How well do these terms match the terminology and definitions presented in this chapter and in Chapter 1?

7. Why is it important to maintain heritage languages? What are the advantages?

Notes

1 This excerpt is from item 23 of Benjamin Franklin's 1751 *Observations Concerning the Increase of Mankind*: "And since Detachments of English from Britain sent to America, will have their Places at Home so soon supply'd and increase so largely here; why should the Palatine Boors be suffered to swarm into our Settlements, and by herding together establish their Language and Manners to the Exclusion of ours? Why should Pennsylvania, founded by the English, become a Colony of *Aliens*, who will shortly be so numerous as to Germanize us instead of our Anglifying them, and will never adopt our Language or Customs, any more than they can acquire our Complexion."

2 There is disagreement and controversy as to the most acceptable term. First Nation, Native American, American Indian, and Indian are all in use by some one or more tribes. As for names of individual languages, there has been a trend to use the tribe's own name, for example, Diné instead of Navajo.

3 The Center for Applied Linguistics (CAL) was founded in 1959 in Washington DC. CAL has an international reputation for its "contributions to the fields of bilingual and dual language education, English as a second language, world languages education, language policy, assessment, immigrant and refugee integration, literacy, dialect studies, and the education of linguistically and culturally diverse adults and children" (http://www.cal.org/who-we-are).

References and Recommended Readings

Adger, C.T., & Christian, D. (2006). Applied social dialectology. In: Ammon, U., Dittmar, N., Mattheier, K.J., & Trudgill, P. (Eds.). *Sociolinguistics: An International Handbook of the Science of Language and Society*. Berlin-New York: Walter De Gruyter.

American Fact Finder. US Census Bureau. https://factfinder.census.gov/faces/tableservices/jsf/pages/productview.xhtml?pid=ACS_16_5YR_S1601&prodType=table.

Blackhorse, A. (2015). Do You Prefer 'Native American' or 'American Indian'? *Indian Country Today*. https://newsmaven.io/indiancountrytoday/archive/blackhorse-do-you-prefer-native-american-or-american-indian-kHWRPJqIGU6X3FTVdMi9EQ/.

Bourhis, R.Y., & Marshall, D.E. (1999). The United States and Canada. In: Joshua Fishman (Ed.), *Handbook of Language and Ethnic Identity* (pp. 244–264). New York: Oxford University Press.

Bowern, C. (2008). *Linguistics Fieldwork: A Practical Guide*. New York: Palgrave-Macmillan Publishers.

Canadian Office of the Commissioner of Official Languages. Official Language Act. www.officiallanguages.gc.ca/en/language_rights/act (Retrieved July 20, 2018).

Carnie, A. (1996). Modern Irish: A Case Study in Language Revival Failure. *MIT Working Papers in Linguistics*. 28: 99–114.

European Union Commission Special Eurobarometer 386 Report: Europeans and Their languages (2012). ec.europa.eu/commfrontoffice/publicopinion/archives/ebs/ebs_386_en.pdf.

Fishman, J., Nahirny, V., Hofman, J., & Hayden, R. (1966). *Language Loyalty in the United States*. The Hague: Mouton.

Franklin, B. (1751). Observations on the increase of mankind. https://founders.archives.gov/documents/Franklin/01-04-02-0080.

Fuller, J.M. (2015). Language choices and ideologies in the bilingual classroom. In: J. Cenoz, D. Gorter (Eds.), *Multilingual Education: Between Language Learning and Translanguaging* (pp. 137–258). Cambridge, MA: Cambridge University Press.

Gill, M. (2016). *The Rosetta Stone*. Ontario Museum of Archeology. archaeologymuseum.ca/the-rosetta-stone/ (Retrieved July 2018).

Gorter, D., Zenotz, V., & Cenoz, J. (Eds.). (2014). *Minority Languages and Multilingual Education: Bridging the Local and the Global*. Dordrecht, the Netherlands: Springer.

Grosjean, F. (2010). *Bilingual: Life and Reality*. Cambridge, MA: Harvard University Press.

Kelleher, A. (2010). What is a Heritage Language? www.cal.org/heritage/pdfs/briefs/What-is-a-Heritage-Language.pdf. Published by Center for Applied Linguistics. (Retrieved July 2018).

Lambert, W.E., Hodgson, R.C., Gardner, R.C., & Fillenbaum, S. (1960). Evaluational reactions to spoken languages. *Journal of Abnormal and Social Psychology.* 20(1): 44–51.

Mahootian, S., Kaplan-Weinger, J., Gebhardt, L., & Hallett, R.W. (2017). *Language and Human Behavior: Topics in Linguistics.* Dubuque, IA: Kendall-Hunt Publishers.

Michaud, C. (2012). English the preferred language for world business: Poll. https://www.reuters.com/article/us-language/english-the-preferred-language-for-world-business-poll-idUSBRE84F0OK20120516 (Retrieved July 10, 2018).

Neeley, T. (2012). Global business speaks English. *Harvard Business Review.* https://hbr.org/2012/05/global-business-speaks-english.

Parkinson, R.B., Diffie, W., & Simpson, R.S. (1999). *Cracking Codes: The Rosetta Stone and Decipherment.* Berkley, CA: University of California Press.

Potowski, K. (Ed.). (2010). *Language Diversity in the USA.* Cambridge, MA: Cambridge University Press.

Ray, J.D. (2007). *The Rosetta Stone and the Rebirth of Ancient Egypt.* Harvard University Press. ISBN 978-0-674-02493-9 (Retrieved June 12, 2018).

Report of the International Expert Group Meeting on Indigenous Languages. (2008). UN Document Symbol: E/C.19/2008/3. United Nations Permanent Forum on Indigenous Issues www.un.org/esa/socdev/unpfii/documents/Factsheet_languages_FINAL.pdf.

Romaine, S. (2013). The bilingual and multilingual community. In: T.K. Bhatia, & W.C. Ritchie (Eds.), *The Handbook of Bilingualism and Multilingualism* (pp. 445–464). Wiley-Blackwell.

Rumbaut, R.G., & Massey, D.S. (2013). Immigration and language diversity in the United States. *Daedalus.* 142(3): 141–154.

Schendl, H., & Wright, L. (Eds.). (2012). *Code-Switching in Early English.* Berlin, Germany: De Gruyter Mouton.

The World Factbook. https://www.cia.gov/library/publications/the-world-factbook/geos/pp.html. (July 10, 2019)

Tiersma, P.M. (2010). Language policy in the United States. In: L. Solan, & P. Tiersma (Eds.), *Oxford Handbook of Language and Law*; Loyola-LA Legal Studies Paper No. 2010-52. SSRN: https://ssrn.com/abstract=1710224 or doi: 10.2139/ssrn.1710224.

UNESCO. (2017). Biodiversity and linguistic diversity: Maintaining Indigenous languages, conserving biodiversity. www.unesco.org/new/en/culture/themes/endangered-languages/biodiversity-and-linguistic-diversity/.

UNESCO Ad Hoc Expert Group on Endangered Languages (2003) . Language Vitality and endangerment. http://www.unesco.org/new/fileadmin/MULT IMEDIA/HQ/CLT/pdf/Language_vitality_and_endangerment_EN.pdf.

US Census. (2019). https://www.census.gov/data/tables/2013/demo/2009-2013-lang-tables.html.

US Census. (2018). www.census.gov/quickfacts/fact/table/US/POP815216# viewtop (Retrieved July 31, 2018).

Warhol, L. (2011). Native American language policy. Center for Applied Linguistics. www.cal.org/heritage/pdfs/briefs/native-american-language-policy.pdf.

World Encyclopedia. *Native North American languages*. www.encyclopedia. com/environment/encyclopedias-almanacs-transcripts-and-maps/native-north-american-languages (Retrieved July 28, 2018 from Encyclopedia. com).

Sites and Videos to Learn More about Endangered Languages and Documentation Efforts

Plains Indian Sign Language. Go to www.youtube.com/watch?v=bfT2a5SG-DFA to see Plains Indian Sign Language (PISL) being used during the 1930 Indian Sign Language Conference. The council was held between General Hugh L. Scott and representatives from 12 Plains Indian tribes, including the Cheyenne, the Sioux, and the Mandan tribes.

The Linguists. (2008). Directed by: Jeremy Newberger, Seth Kramer and Daniel A. Miller. Ironbound Films.

First Language – The Race to Save Cherokee (2014). The Cherokee Indians fight to restore their native language in this award-winning documentary. (DVD, Length 56 minutes). www.youtube.com/watch?v=e9y8fDOLsO4

Language Keepers: The Struggle for Indigenous Language Survival in California. (2016). The last speakers of a number of Indigenous languages of California discuss their efforts to revitalize their endangered languages. https://emergencemagazine.org/story/language-keepers/#/

Chapter 3

Mixing Languages
Structure and Social Functions

We have thus far looked at the development of bilingualism and how it can affect individuals and societies. In this chapter, we will look at how speakers combine two (or more) languages and produce mixed grammatical phrases and discourse (codeswitches). We will discover that the language choices the bilingual makes (monolingual LA or LB, or mixed LA-LB), whether intentional or unintentional, can be meaningful. We also learn about the attitudes of monolinguals and bilinguals toward codeswitching.

Although, at one time, it was believed these mixes occurred randomly, over the last six decades studies have shown that language mixing (codeswitching) is a systematic rule-governed linguistic behavior. Switching may be conscious and intentional or unconscious and unintentional. Intentional switching may be used to indicate shifts in topic, or to redirect the conversation to a different person (interlocutor) in the conversation. Speakers may also switch languages intentionally to signal a change in interpersonal or social relationships, to make the conversation more intimate or to make it more formal. It may also be used to position oneself as an insider or an outsider with respect to a social or ethnic community, to index and communicate identity, and to enhance social and political statements. Much of the time, however, switching between languages/dialects is unintentional, a result of psycho- and sociolinguistic variables that the speaker is not consciously aware of, involving processing issues and the tendency of speakers to adapt their speech style to the interlocutor's style and/or community norms and expectations. Although switching has at times been associated with the loss of one language, many researchers believe that codeswitching is a natural consequence of ability and competence in more than one language and, accordingly, should not automatically be regarded as language deficit, loss, or shift. As discussed in previously, language shift or loss is a result of multiple social variables (i.e., lack of support for the speech community, lack of valorization of the language, etc.). In this chapter, we learn more about using multiple-language discourse, choosing between languages, and the social and grammatical rules that guide switches and choices.

3.1 Managing Multiple Languages

We know that all languages have grammars, rules that guide speakers to produce well-structured, acceptable sentences and steer them away from generating unacceptable utterances. Some of these rules are overtly taught, but most are learned as we progress through the various stages of language acquisition that begin in infancy. So what happens when the brain has more than one grammatical system to manage? To start our investigation, let's begin with some fundamental terms, definitions, and examples.

Code—In the context of bilingualism, code refers to languages and their varieties. Therefore, Japanese is a code as is Hebrew, French, Thai, and so on.

Codeswitching—Codeswitching, also written as code-switching, refers to the act of changing from one language or dialect to another. It can be defined as the systematic use of two or more languages or varieties of the same language during oral or written discourse. It's a common speech behavior, most often used in informal, casual contexts. Codeswitching can occur **intrasententially**, within a sentence, including the switching of a single word, prefix, or suffix. It can also occur **intersententially**, between sentences at the discourse level. Both types of switches can and do occur in spoken and written communications.

Codeswitches—Codeswitches (or code-switches) are the result of codeswitching; this term refers to utterances and discourse that contain more than one language or dialect.

Codemixing—Although in the past some scholars have made a distinction between codemixing (or code-mixing) and codeswitching, in most current literature, codemixing and codeswitching are used interchangeably (Mahootian, 2006). Here, too, I will be doing the same.

Mixed-code—This term refers to the language variety available to bilingual speakers during discourse (written or spoken) which includes codeswitches. The basic premise is that bilinguals have three codes/ language varieties to choose from during discourse. For example, a Kurdish-English speaker can choose to speak monolingual Kurdish or English, or a mix of the two. In the third option, the speaker allows herself to use Kurdish-English codeswitches.

The next section presents some examples of intrasentential and intersentential codeswitches between various language pairs.[1] In all the examples, a switch into the other language is shown by underlining the word or phrase that has been switched into. For example, in a switch from English to Arabic, the Arabic text will be underlined. The first line of each example is the codeswitched phrase, the second line shows a literal word-by-word translation of the non-English words, and the third line is a translation of the entire phrase or sentence into natural English. The hyphen seen in some words indicates a bound morpheme (bound morphemes are meaningful bits of language that cannot stand alone and must be attached to another morpheme like the English past tense marker *–ed* in walk**ed** or the plural marker *–s* in crumb**s**). ACC = accusative marker (object of verb). TOP = topic marker, which indicates the topic of a sentence and often overlaps with the subject of the sentence. English does not use topic markers. Japanese and Korean are among a few languages that do. Language names have also been abbreviated as follows; Eng = English, Sp = Spanish, Ar = Arabic, Fr = French, Ir = Irish, Jap= Japanese, and Pers = Persian.

3.1.1 Intrasentential Codeswitches

(1) I have no idea <u>laesh he sot keetha</u>.
          _____ why she did that.
    'I have no idea why she did that'   (Eng-Ar)

(2) Tiene que estar en la <u>court hearing</u>.
    She/he has to be in the _____
    'She/he has to be in the court hearing.'   (Sp-Eng)

(3) Ana <u>already</u> jebtaha.
    I _____ brought it
    'I already brought it.'   (Ar-Eng)

(4) The color of the <u>tapete</u> is red.
    _____ rug _____
    'The color of the rug is red.'   (Eng-Sp)

(5) Tu peux aller a <u>Michigan Avenue</u>.
    You can go to _____
    'You can go to Michigan Avenue.'   (Fr-Eng)

(6) Beidh an jackpot anocht a'ainn.
    Will be the _____ tonight do
    'We'll get the jackpot tonight.'   (Ir-Eng, Laoire, 2016)

(7) one algebra question-<u>o</u> mark <u>shite</u>
    _____ACC. __ do
    'you mark one algebra question'   (Eng-Jap, Nishimura, 1985)

(8) un professeur <u>a Dim</u>
    a professor excellent
    'an excellent professor'   (Fr-Ar, Bentahila & Davies, 1983)

(9) inta hang-<u>ha</u> up
    You ____ -it __
    'you hang it up'   (Ar-Eng, Mohammed, 1983)

(10) job-<u>anna</u>
      -PL
    'jobs'   (Ir-Eng, Stenson, 1990)

(11) She-<u>wa</u> took her a month to come home-<u>yo</u>.
       TOP
    'As for her, (it) took her a month to come home, you know.'
               (Eng-Jap, Nishimura, 1985)

(12) Lawyer-<u>et</u> will tell you what to do.
    _____-your _____
    'Your lawyer will tell you what to do.'
               (Eng-Pers, Mahootian, 1993)

(13) Hay frases que lusen más <u>cool</u> en inglés.
    There-are phrases that seem more ___ in English.
    'There are phrases that seem cooler in English.'   (Sp-Eng)

(14) I'm planting red <u>shamduni</u> this time.
    _____ geranium(s)_____
    'I'm planting red <u>geraniums</u> this time.'   (Eng-Pers)

(15) acum lucr.ez în <u>turn</u>-ul de noapte.
    now work I in shift-the of night
    'Now I work the night shift.'   (Rom-Sp, Munteanu, 2007)

(16) The <u>yamcha</u> took my job.
      backstabber
    'The backstabber took my job.'   (Kor-Eng)

> **Thinking Matters**
>
> Take another look at the 16 examples of codeswitches. What parts of speech are switched (nouns, verbs, adjectives, adverbs, etc.)? What else do you notice?

You may have detected that all categories of words were involved with switches, from nouns to adjectives, adverbs, and verbs. You may have also noticed that a number of closed-class items were involved with switches (e.g., articles, prepositions, tense markers, possessives), and both free morphemes (words that are meaningful without any additional prefixes or suffixes) and bound morphemes (morphemes that must be attached to something).

3.1.2 Intersentential

The next two example sentences show intersentential switches. Though less frequent than intrasentential single-word switches, this type of switching is common. At times, the switch is guided by a change in topic, or for the sake of accommodating the speaker's or hearer's stronger language. The change can also be a means of intentionally distancing the speaker from the topic or connecting the speaker more closely to the hearer. We will discuss motivations for intentional switching in the next section. In the example in (17), the speaker is trying to reassure the hearer by switching to the home language. In (18), the speaker uses a phrase that she commonly says to her husband. She feels that saying 'do what you want' in Spanish sounds less harsh than in English. She really does want her husband to do whatever he wants, so in this case she uses Spanish to establish more of a connection, so that he does not become offended, or take it the wrong way.[2]

(17) I called him last night. <u>Be maen goft se miyad</u>.
                           . to me said three will come
    'I called him last night. He said he'll come at three.'   (Eng-Pers)

(18) I don't know. <u>Haz lo que quieras</u>.
      _____. Do you that you want.
   'I don't know. Do what you want.'

                             (Eng-Sp)

Borrowing—Borrowings, also referred to as **loan words**, are any words or phrases taken from one language and used by monolingual speakers of another language. Frequently, borrowings fill lexical gaps arising from imported concepts resulting from cultural contact through trade, conquest, and immigration. As a rule, newly introduced concepts and items are accompanied by their names. Now, it happens that because not all languages have all the same sounds and sound combinations, once a word is borrowed, the pronunciation changes to adapt to the sounds of the host language. An example, the word *taxi* when borrowed into Japanese is pronounced *takushee*, thus obeying the Japanese sound combination rule that makes the combination of sound 's' followed by the sound 'e' into 'shee'; also since Japanese doesn't allow two consonant sounds together, the Japanese pronunciation inserts 'u' between the 'k' sound and the 'sh' sound. Additionally, using borrowings sometimes imparts a different message than if the same word is used in the host language. For example, the English words *babysitter*, *nationalism*, and *bargain* are used in Japanese when a speaker wants to reverse or downplay the negative connotations of the Japanese equivalents.

Another interesting example of borrowing comes from an unexpected source—the use of *shitstorm* by Chancellor Angela Merkel in a televised speech on December 3, 2018. Apparently, German does not have a word for this useful and graphic term, even though German has its own words for "shit" and "storm". Though the German language can convey the same message, it doesn't have a lexical item (one word) that captures the concept as succinctly; instead, German has borrowed the term from English. And, as often happens with borrowings of abstract words, some aspect of the word is left behind when it is borrowed. In this case, it is the vulgarity of the word that is left behind. For Germans, 'shitstorm' is not a vulgar word, but merely a strong description of the media avalanche an event causes. The word has been part of the German lexicon and has been listed in the Duden dictionary (a standard German dictionary) since 2013.[3]

English, in turn, has borrowed from German and Japanese. Can you think of any Japanese words you can find in English-language dictionaries? Here are some German and Japanese words you may be familiar with—German: *kindergarten, iceberg, wunderkind, angst, uber-*(as a prefix, not the transportation company), *doppelganger, poltergeist*; Japanese: *futon, manga, karaoke, sushi, emoji, edamame*. Put the words through a translator to listen to the native pronunciation. What do you notice? Do you pronounce them in the same way?

Actually, English is filled with words from other languages, borrowed over centuries. Some have come into the language through wars, others through commerce. Latin and French are two of the major sources of borrowings into English. Latin has given us words such as *plant, pear, organ, bishop, heretic, pot*, and *cook*, along with a large percentage of our medical and scientific terminology. French contributed words related to food, fashion, government, and law, such as *cardinal, duke, court, abbey, beef, mutton, joy, poor*, and *fruit*. English has also borrowed from Arabic (e.g., *orange, algebra, apricot, alcohol, artichoke, coffee, lemon, admiral*), Hebrew (e.g., *jubilee, cider, golem, challah, cherub*), Persian (e.g., *paradise, bronze, bazaar, borax, crimson*), Spanish (e.g., *patio, plaza, buckaroo, alfalfa, pinto*), and Native American languages (e.g., *caribou* from Míkmaq, *caucus* is the Algonquian word for "counsel" or "advisor", *chipmunk* originally was 'chitmunk' from Odawa).

It's important to note that borrowings are distinguished from codeswitches by the fact that they have become part of the monolingual lexicon—they can be found in monolingual dictionaries of the borrowers and are readily used by monolinguals. For instance, one doesn't need to be a speaker of Spanish to know what a *taco* is or know Míkmaq to know what *caribou* refers to, and to use these words in a sentence.

Thinking Matters

Look up the following words to discover from which languages they were borrowed into English: *balcony, ketchup, graffiti, kiwi, pajamas, messiah, malice, maternal, robot, tattoo, vitamin, whiskey.*

3.1.3 Intentional and Unintentional Codeswitching

There are a number of reasons for bilinguals to codeswitch. Many linguists have observed that switching from one language/dialect to another is pragmatically similar to style shifting in monolingual discourse. For example, as monolinguals, we have a continuum of styles to employ during discourse, from casual speech to formal to ceremonial speech styles. Each of these styles can be finely tuned to fit the audience we address (e.g., a professor, parents, friends, younger sibling), and the occasion and context of the discourse (e.g., in public, at home, on a social media platform). For each encounter, we choose the appropriate style—level of formality, use of slang, topic of conversation, etc. For example, casual speech to address your six-year-old will be different from the casual style you use with your peers. We also shift styles when we write an academic paper, a short story, a birthday card, an email, a tweet, or a letter home. Most of the time, these style shifts happen automatically, without any conscious decision making on the part of the speaker: we don't really need to think whether it's OK to use the f-word with grandma when describing the great time we had at the Lollapalooza music festival or wonder if our toddler would enjoy an OpEd from the *Washington Post* for a bedtime story.

For bilinguals, codeswitching, like style shifting, can be unconscious, as part of the cultural and pragmatic knowledge acquired as members of speech communities. But codeswitching can also be conscious and intentional. Unintentional switches are often motivated by a combination of linguistic and psycholinguistic issues. For instance, lexical gaps in the speaker's lexicon in one language can automatically call up the needed word in the other language. To illustrate, a Swahili-French speaker may know how to say 'orchard' in Swahili (*bustani*) but not in French (*verger*). Consequently when this speaker is in conversation with other Swahili-French bilinguals he or she will use *bustani* to refer to an orchard, even if the conversation is in French. Unintentional switches may also have a psycholinguistic source based on the frequency of the speaker's use of each word in each language. If the word is used more frequently in Language A than it is in Language B, in the course of keeping the conversation fluid without lengthy pauses to find the word in LB, LA will come to the rescue, more or less seamlessly, and often without conscious knowledge or effort on the part of the speaker. The example from the Punjabi-English speaker in (19) exemplifies some of the linguistic and cognitive outcomes of unintentional switching and offers a peek into one of the social dimensions of codeswitching, that of attitudes regarding language mixing in some communities.

(19) I mean I'm guilty in that sense <u>ke ziada wsi</u> English <u>i bolde fer ode nal eda</u> … <u>wsi</u> mix <u>kerde rene ã</u>. I mean, unconsciously, subconsciously, <u>keri jane e</u> …

'I mean I'm guilty in that sense that we speak English more and more … we keep mixing.

I mean unconsciously, subconsciously, we keep doing it …'
(Romaine, 1995, p. 122)

The effortless, unconscious switches from one language to the other have interesting implications for theories of syntax and for theories of language storage, organization, and access in the brain. In Section 3.8 of this chapter, "Mechanisms: The Rules of Codeswitching," we review the various models proposed to account for the grammatical structure of code-mixed utterances, and in Chapter 5 we learn about other psycholinguistic theories proposed to account for codeswitching.

Of special interest to sociolinguists are instances of intentional switching when speakers deliberately choose one language or variety rather than the other during discourse. Intentional codeswitching is an altogether different communicative behavior. Every word, hesitation, sentence style (active or passive, direct or indirect)—every tone we use is meaningful, so it's not surprising that for bilinguals, *which* language is used will also be telling, signaling its own message. In the next sections, we will investigate the *intent* behind intentional codewitching and the relationship between language choice and identity. We will also discover why some researchers talk about language as a resource in multilingual contexts.

3.2 Conversational Functions of Codeswitching

Codeswitching, especially when intentional, is a discourse tool with many functions. Purposeful codeswitching can occur in speech or in writing. In either mode, there is a meta-message, an extra layer of information which speaks to a complex of social, psychological, and political variables that guide individual and societal behaviors. For example, the extra message may be something as simple as playfulness, mixed with a bit of modernity and youthfulness, such as the following switch to the English progressive suffix *-ing* in this otherwise all-Chinese utterance:

(20) 第一天上班，混日子 ing (Chinese-English, Luqun Ge, 2007)
di yi tian shang ban, hunrizi ___
first day at work, muddle (ing) along
'(This is my) first day at work and (I am) just muddling along.'

Of the use of the bound morpheme *-ing* instead of the equivalent Chinese morpheme *zhong*, Sonya Chen, a trilingual Chinese-American in Chicago, notes that it is

> interesting to see nowadays a lot of the younger generation like to use *-ing* to represent present tense, and I've seen people do this mostly in typing, not so much in speech. I am not sure why, but as I take away the *-ing* and replace it with its Chinese counterpart *zhong*, it seems *zhong* makes it sound more formal, but when using *-ing*, it sounds informal and fun.

Chen's observation corroborates Luqun Ge's claim that the use of *–ing* in his data "makes the conversation funny and exotic, which I think, is a big feature of the BBS [Bulletin Board] computer-mediated discourse" (2007, p. 39).

Whether we speak one language or multiple languages, we are all aware of the sociocultural norms of our speech communities, many of which are coded and delivered through some property of language. We know how to be snarky or how to be sweet by merely altering a word, a tone, a gesture. We're mindful of the deadly consequences of a hesitation before answering a question like "How do I look?" or "Does this make me look fat?" Now imagine having more than one language at your disposal. Aside from the ability to communicate with monolingual and bilingual speakers of each language, bilinguals have an extra tool or resource to utilize: with two or more languages in the bilingual's repertoire, which language is used or whether to use mixed code or not becomes a complex decision, with numerous social implications. Whether in face-to-face conversation, or in literature, magazines, poems, advertising, and other media, or in the in-between of blogs, computer-mediated conversations, tweets, messaging, and other social media, intentional switching has a purpose that goes beyond the meaning of the words and sentences. So while some linguists were working out the syntactic features of codeswitching, others were looking for systematic ways to describe the functions of codeswitching, especially when switching was by choice. In one of the earliest attempts to capture uniformity, Gumperz posited six conversational functions of intentional codeswitching (Gumperz, 1982, p. 75–78):

(a) *Quotation*: to distinguish between direct speech and quotations or reported speech: When quoting or reporting someone, speakers will often switch into the language the person used, as in the Persian-English example in (21) (Mahootian et al., 2017, p. 156) and the French-English example in (22):

(21) unvaeqt John be maen mige, "<u>I don't think I can make it.</u>"
then John to me says _____
'Then John says to me, "I don't think I can make it."'

(22) 'c'était bruyant mais je pense qu'elle a dit <u>"can I have your number?"</u>
It was noisy but I think that she said _____
'It was noisy but I think she said "can I have your number?"'

(b) *Addressee specification*: speakers may switch between languages to address a message to a specific person in a conversation, as in the following Persian-English example adapted from Mahootian et al. (2017, p. 156), where three friends are talking: A bilingual Iranian Persian-English speaker; an Iranian Persian-English, Hearer 1(H1); and an American monolingual English speaker, Hearer 2(H2).

(23) 'Well I don't know how to describe it but it just doesn't feel like home to me' (directed to H1 and H2). '<u>To miduni maenzuraem chie, doroste?</u> (you know what I mean, right?' directed to H1).

(c) *Interjection/sentence fillers*: speakers may codeswitch interjections or sentence fillers such as 'you know', 'know what I mean?' Spanish *eh* and *ay* (to intensify or draw attention) and *mira* and *fijate* ('look' and 'notice', respectively, to draw attention to a point being made), Japanese *neh*?, Persian *doroste*? (right?), and Hebrew *oy/oy vay* (as a disheartened response).

(24) <u>Ay</u>! you have to read the directions BEFORE assembling it.

(d) *Reiteration*: speakers may switch languages to emphasize or clarify a message, as in the Spanish-English example in (25), the Hindi-English example from Gumperz (1982, p. 78) in (26), and the English-Croatian example in (27):

(25) Hey, how are you? <u>como te va todo</u>?

                  How you goes everything?

'Hey, how are you? How's everything going?'

(26) Father in India calling to his son who was learning to swim in a swimming pool, first in Hindi and then repeated in English:

Baju-me jao beta, andar mat. <u>Keep to the side.</u>

Go to the side son, not inside. _____

'Go to the side son, not inside. Keep to the side.'

(27) Mom, <u>ide</u>! Let's go home.

_____ (let's)go _____

'Mom, let's go! Let's go home.'

(e) *Message qualification*: speakers may switch to add more information in order to qualify the main message, as in the following Slovenian-German and English-Spanish examples (from Gumperz, 1982, p. 60 and 79, respectively).

(28) Uzeymas ti kafe? <u>Oder te</u>?

'Will you take coffee? Or tea?'

(29) The oldest one, la grande la de once años

_____, the big one who is eleven years old.

'The oldest one, the big one who is eleven years old.'

(f) *Personalization versus objectification*: in this category, switching marks a number of related functions that reflect the degree of speaker involvement or distancing vis-à-vis the message, the interlocutors, etc., as we saw in earlier examples (16 and 17), repeated here in (30) and (31).

(30) I called him last night. <u>Be maen goft se miyad</u>.

                  to me said three will come

'I called him last night. He said he'll come at three.' (Eng-Pers)

(31) I don't know. <u>Haz lo que quieras</u>.
     Do you that you want.
  'I don't know. Do what you want.' (Eng-Sp)

Since Gumperz's seminal work, as the field continues to investigate the complex nature of language choice, many of the codeswitching functions he proposed have been recast and extended by other linguists to include the following:

(g) To keep conversations private in public spaces or exclude others from a conversation. Can you think of contexts where this type of switching might occur?

(h) To avoid awkward, meaningless translation of idioms and cultural concepts such as the English-Korean sentence in (32), where translation of the word *baek-il* would be devoid of the significance of this cultural ritual, and the Dutch-Turkish example in (33) from Eversteijn (2011):

(32) We are celebrating the child's <u>baek-il</u>
  ———————————————— one hundredth day.
 'We are celebrating the child's one hundredth day.'

(33) Ben je naar die <u>dügün</u> geweest?
 Have you been to that <u>wedding party</u>?
 In the monolingual context of Turkish, Eversteijn explains, 'dügün' ('wedding') is not a highly specific word. However, in the bilingual context of the Netherlands, the word 'dügün' has the connotation of a wedding according to Turkish traditions, while its Dutch equivalent 'bruiloft' is associated with a wedding according to Dutch traditions. Because of this connotation of Turkishness, 'dügün' becomes a culturally evocative term in the bilingual context. The use of dügün' includes the cultural assumptions, emotional overtones, subjective interpretation, sociocultural values, and ideological assumptions of Turkish cultural values.

(i) To raise the status of the speaker and/or add authority or expertise to a message. This function is illustrated in the following excerpt from an exchange between a passenger and a bus driver in Nairobi, where Swahili is the lingua franca. In this situation, Swahili is also the socially expected choice, and English, which is the prestige/professional/authority language, is the unexpected choice (Scotton & Ury, 1977, pp. 16–17). The conversation begins in Swahili and ends in English. Scotton and Ury interpret the passenger's switch to English as an attempt to pull rank and assert authority. The English translations of the Swahili are in parentheses.

(34) Setting: A conductor on a Nairobi bus has asked a passenger where he is going in order to determine the fare (in Swahili).

Passenger (Swahili): Nataka kwenda posta. (I want to go to the post office.)

Conductor (Swahili): Kutoka hapa mpaka posta nauli ni senti hamsini. (From here to the post the fare is 50 cents.)

(Passenger gives conductor a shilling from which there should be 50 cents in change)

Conductor (Swahili): Ngojea change yako. (Wait for your change.)

(Passenger says nothing until a few minutes have passed and the bus nears the post office where the passenger will get off.)

Passenger (Swahili): Nataka change yangu. (I want my change.)

Conductor (Swahili): Change utapata, Bwana. (You'll get your change, mister.)

Passenger (English): I am nearing my destination.

Conductor (English): Do you think I could run away with your change?

(j)   For creating humorous, playful effects, as in the Chinese utterance presented earlier in example (20).

(k)   To soften a statement, as in Basque to Spanish example in (35). Muñoa Barredo explains that here the switching is a means of adding affection to the exchange.

The speaker uses a Spanish idiomatic expression to refer to his sister's weight. Had he continued using the Basque term (*potola*: 'fat'), the result of his utterance would have been much stronger and with negative connotations. The Spanish idiomatic expression adds a loving tone to what he is saying and makes the other participants laugh.

(Muñoa Barredo, 1997)

(35) bai, bai, o sea, oronda y lironda!
   'right, right, I mean, a little butter ball!'

(l) To change the topic or make side comments. For example, a Korean-English speaker who has received all of their higher education in English would most likely switch to English when talking about their area of study.

(m) To mark group or personal identity and/or emphasize solidarity and camaraderie. This function has received much attention in the recent years. In the following sections, we look at language choice, including the choice of mixed code varieties, as social and/or political statements of individual and community identification, solidarity, and empowerment.

3.3 Language Choice and Codeswitching as Identity and Resource

Language clearly intertwines powerfully with conceptions and definitions of allegiance and 'belonging'. It possesses more than instrumental value; it is the vehicle of tradition and culture, and the medium of group narrative. Issues of psychology and sociology, of symbol and subjectivity, become important whenever we observe language in society. When more than one language is involved, then, we should expect ramifications in terms of identity and 'groupness'.

(John Edwards, 2013, p. 20)

People do not possess one identity related to the social categories to which they belong, but rather they present and re-present themselves, choosing within an inventory of more or less compatible identities that intersect and or contrast with each other in different ways and in accordance with changing social circumstances and interlocutors.

(Anna De Fina, 2007, p. 353)

Thinking Matters

Take a moment to write a definition of identity. Then write a few sentences in which you describe your identity.

We can carry identity cards. We can have our identity stolen. We can have an identity crisis. So what is identity? Ask the question and you'll get answers ranging from legal definitions such as the information on drivers' licenses and passports, to a list of attributes endowed by one's DNA (e.g., brown-eyed six-foot-five redhead), or educational attainments (e.g., high school graduate, sophomore in college, linguistics major) and professions (e.g., biologist, sanitation engineer, professor, ballerina). Some make reference to their gender or sexual orientation (e.g., transgender, gay, cisgender, bisexual, male, female), habits (e.g., morning person, six-cups-a-day coffee drinker), hobbies (e.g., rock climber, stamp collector, gardening enthusiast), ethnicity (e.g., Asian, Caucasian, Latinx, Hispanic, African-American), nationality (e.g., Yemenite, Nigerian, Polish, Welsh), and religious beliefs (e.g., Buddhist, atheist, Episcopalian, Shiite, Hindu). What this tells us is that identity is not a monolithic static construction. Rather, it is a dynamic, malleable assembly, a record of our experiences, ideologies, and beliefs, all of which can be expressed through language. Interestingly, in their responses to the identity question, individuals don't normally include the language(s) they speak as a descriptor of who they are.

Yet research and researchers have determined time and again that language is, in fact, a substantial part of national and personal identities. Language is equated with nation and nationality, with heritage and culture. The refrain "how can you be X-nationality if you don't speak the language of X-nationality?" is often heard by the grandchildren of immigrants in every corner of the world and taken seriously by many younger members of bilingual communities as well. Language is also associated with social status and power. Jørgensen (1998) and Blommaert (2005), among others, suggest that we should view identity in terms of an evolving repertoire which draws from a variety of sources, with language serving as one of the sources for identity construction and social status. Consequently, in this view, a status identity requires a status language.

The relationships between language and identity and language and power become more apparent in multilingual communities where each language and its resulting mixed varieties come with a set of cultural norms, expectations, and values assigned from within and outside of its community of practice. Accordingly, Jørgensen explains, "[S]peakers of some language, or varieties of languages, automatically can expect to wield more [social] power than the speakers of some other languages or varieties, everything else being equal" (p. 237). The exchange in the previous section between the bus driver and passenger in Nairobi in example (34) is a perfect illustration of languages as resources that encode identity and social status. The language choices made by the two speakers are purposeful and strategic, governed by both speakers' knowledge of the status of each language within their community. In his study of Turkish-Danish speaking second, third, and fifth graders in Danish schools, Jørgensen concludes that codeswitching is used to highlight and demonstrate play or solidarity within the children's interpersonal relationships, whether it is to change the topic of conversation or form alliances.

In each of the scenarios in Jørgensen's study, the children were in small groups, working on a project given to them by the researchers. To complete the project, it was necessary for them to talk with each other. The children were aware they were being recorded but didn't know for what purpose, nor did they have access to the tape recorder. Most of the language switching was intersentential, though in some cases single words or short phrases were interjected from one language into the other. In general, Danish was used to talk about the project (the school task), while Turkish was used as the private language to express emotions, or to make other personal comments. For example, not surprisingly, swearing and other derogatory comments were made in Turkish.

In another study, of Turkish-Dutch speakers in the Netherlands, Eversteijn (2011) found similar patterns of codeswitching and language choice identified in other studies of other language pairs and age groups. In her survey of 50 Turkish-Dutch bilingual teens between 11 and 19 years of age, her participants reported choosing one language over the other to establish or maintain a connection, to assert status, to include or exclude others, or to assert identity. Eversteijn used a multifaceted methodological approach combining analysis of self-reports and conversational analysis. She found that balanced bilingual Turkish-Dutch teenagers apply language choice and codeswitching extensively to either converge with or diverge from their interlocutors. The teens exploited the principles of convergence and divergence in very subtle ways. For example, they understood that a message with unpleasant or dispreferred overtones can either be aggravated by using someone's dominant language or softened by using the listener's non-dominant language. In the example that follows, Dutch is in italics. In the example, a teenage girl reports how she addresses her mother, who is dominant in Turkish:

1. When my mother is telling me that I cannot wear certain clothes when we are going somewhere, I will say (in Dutch) *wat gaat jou dat aan*? (That is none of your business, is it?)

Eversteijn concludes that by answering in Dutch, her mother's non-dominant language, the teen softens the tone and content of an otherwise rude response.

Auer and Dirmi (2003) found still another interesting display of codeswitching used to gain access to a group (to belong) or to distance the speakers from a group. They report on the acquisition of Turkish by young, non-Turkish Germans of various language backgrounds in Hamburg. They conclude that the use of Turkish has two functions: (1) it allows the users to mix with the other Turkish speakers (ethnic Turks), and (2) it serves as their own in-group non-mainstream, subculture language even when ethnic Turks are not present, to set them apart from other groups. Altogether, we can see that although language pairs and speakers' ages and community locations may differ, the functions of codeswitching are finite, and it is possible to account for the codeswitches in a uniform manner.

3.3.1 Cultural Codeswitching

We have read at length about the forms and functions of codeswitching. Recently, there has been talk about codeswitching to accommodate *cultural* expectations. Called "cultural codeswitching", it has been part of the social reality of many speakers of regional dialects cross-culturally for a very long time. As we discussed in the section on attitudes toward bilingualism (2.3), attitudes toward languages and their varieties are about the speakers, not what they are speaking. Add race and color to the equation, and the pressures speakers face are not merely about what opinion someone may have about them based on their speech, but are about how those opinions are accompanied by prejudicial, discriminatory judgments and harmful actions.

More and more speakers in the US, especially those in African-American communities, are, in one way or other, speaking up and out about the pressure to conform. Like the immigrants who feel pressured to acquire English in order to show they are good citizens, many African-Americans feel the same pressures to talk "White". Speakers of African-American vernacular English varieties (AAVE) feel pressured to use a standard variety of English in some social and in many work contexts in what is called cultural codeswitching. Many AAVE speakers perceive the expectation to codeswitch to a White variety of English as obligatory. They feel forced into switching to the "standard" code in order to be taken seriously and accepted as culturally compatible with White American culture, and to be a nonthreatening person of color. This one-sided switching further exposes social inequalities based on race and imposed through language. Sociologist Chandra Waring writes:

> [B]ecause [the] dominant culture is white, whiteness has been baked into institutions as natural, normal and legitimate. So there's much more incentive for people of color to code-switch – to adapt to the dominant culture to improve their prospects. White people rarely, if ever, feel this same pressure in their daily lives.
>
> (http://theconversation.com, 2018)

CEO and entrepreneur Chandra Arthur approaches the same question from a slightly different angle. In her 2017 TEDx talk, "The Cost of Code Switching", Ms. Arthur asks who is expected to codeswitch. She maintains that sounding "American" is more than using English. It is using the socially supported variety of English, dressing mainstream, and, in short, being nonthreatening. She also, to an extent and for the time being, encourages AAVE speakers to develop codeswitching abilities. In her talk, Arthur, who is African-American, recalls her unexpected, terrifying brush with police while in her own home. She attributes the quick resolution to what could have been even more disastrous to being able to speak 'White'. She also reminds us of the 2009 incident where Henry Louis Gates Jr., Harvard professor and host of the PBS program "Finding Your Roots" was arrested by Cambridge, Massachusetts, police for breaking and entering when he was merely trying to get into his own home. Yes, it sounds crazy, but it's nevertheless true. In both cases, whether stated explicitly or implied, the police action taken against them was because both Ms. Arthur and Dr. Gates are African-American. Ms. Arthur also stresses that the "costs of [cultural] codeswitching on society are huge because it means those of us who belong to minority language communities spend a lot more time learning the language of cultural compatibility and less time doing the things that matter to all of us".

The following are some examples of cultural codeswitching from the African-American perspective. The comments from viewers are equally eye-opening, as so many admit to how exhausted and pressured they feel to speak 'White'.

Chandra Arthur, *The Cost of Codeswitching*

www.youtube.com/watch?v=Bo3hRq2RnNl

In the 2018 film, *Sorry to Bother You*, Danny Glover gives Cassius advice on how to make money as a telemarketer:

Let me give you a tip. You wanna make some money here? Use your White voice … . I'm not talkin'about Will Smith white … . www.imdb.com/title/tt5688932/videoplayer/vi1982642201? ref_=tt_ov_vi

The next two videos are examples of codeswitching between Black English and White English, as posted by Atlanta Black Star (https://atlantablackstar.com/about-us/) and BuzzfeedCocoa Butter, a venue created 2016 "to distribute more black content", according to Blavity.[4]

www.facebook.com/ATLBlackStar/videos/yall-code-switch/134823 3008644802/

www.facebook.com/BuzzFeedCocoaButter/videos/code-switch ing-101/1279991948798807/?jazoest

Key and Peele video www.youtube.com/watch?v=_YkE7W6qegg

Obama and anger translator https://www.youtube.com/watch? v=HkAK9QRe4ds

There are numerous examples like these, across languages and ages, of speakers who codeswitch in order to accommodate others, to fit in, to protect themselves, or to achieve a social end. However, the concern that has been voiced, and which sets cultural codeswitching apart, is the extent to which speakers of AAVE feel forced to switch, adapt, and be someone other than who they are or want to be.

In the next section, we look at how purposeful language choice is used in written contexts such as newspapers, magazines, novels, computer-mediated communications (CMCs) (e.g., email, text, tweets) and street and storefront signs to explicitly achieve some social goal or to assert a speech community's or individual's identity, political affiliation, and/or ethnicity.

3.4 Code Choice and Codeswitching in Writing

Beyond what we have already learned about the variable status of languages in diglossic communities, examining language choice where there is an imbalance of social status and political power between ethnic minorities and the dominant culture reveals additional extra-linguistic messages that are delivered through language choice. Analysis of code choice and codeswitches in the Spanish-English bilingual women's magazine *Latina* between 1999 and 2002 led me to conclude that the use of mixed code and codeswitches throughout articles and other features was intended to

> evoke a sense of cultural identity, unity and camaraderie, a direct and undeniable assertion of the bilingual identity. It is a way for speakers to underscore their ethnicity, their connection to their heritage and to others who share that heritage and the values associated with it, *within the majority culture and language.*
>
> (Mahootian, 2005, p. 365)

I determined that the use of **Spanglish** (speech or writing that uses a mixture of Spanish and English) in *Latina* is meant to reinforce Spanglish as a speech variety, and more importantly, to reinforce the bicultural Latinx identity (see also Toribio, 2002, 2011).

Thinking Matters

The term *Latinx* has been replacing *Latin@* and its previous form *Latina/o*. Trace the evolution of these words. When and why did each term rise to popular use?

Watch this short YouTube video about Spanglish produced by the Language and Life project: www.youtube.com/

watch?v=nYMnNlfSMC0. Do you know Spanish-English bilinguals who use Spanglish? How about bilinguals of other language pairs?

Two aspects stand out in the codeswitches in *Latina*. The first is that codeswitching is used in a national publication. This immediately elevates codeswitching and the use of a mixed-code variety, in this case Spanglish, to a cool, young, progressive language choice, despite its negative stereotype as 'street talk', 'verbal salad', slang, and so forth. We can safely assume that there is a population that identifies with the magazine's content and format; and given the proportion of English to Spanish in *Latina*, a population dominant in English, with a passive knowledge of Spanish. In fact, *Latina* identifies its mission and target audience as

> 100 percent Latina. 100 percent American. All pride. All passion. This is how Latina Media Ventures (LMV) sees its unique world. And it is what drives the mission to bring the U.S. Latin community the best, most empowering, engaging and culturally relevant content.

And, of their choice to have performer Selena Quintanilla, who died in 1997, as the cover of their November 2016 issue, they write

> Selena rose above the identity struggle by not struggling at all. Instead, she leaned into her Latina-ness and embraced who she so gloriously was: an American-born, non-native-Spanish-speaking Latina who was curvy and brown, and loved both pizza and tacos.
> (www.latina.com/entertainment/celebrity/
> selena-quintanilla-latina-magazine-
> november-2016-cover-star?utm_source
> =social_share&utm)

Their stated mission of serving a 100 percent American, 100 percent Latina population, and their acknowledgment of a Latina identity is further reinforced by the use of mixed code in some of the magazine's feature articles, covers, editorials, and letters to the editor from its readers. What stands out in the codeswitches is that most are single words (nouns, prepositions, adjectives, interjections) or short phrases and idioms, many in elementary Spanish and understandable through context.

Readers are also given a 'heads-up' since all Spanish words are presented in italics, as in the following examples. The sprinkling of Spanish across some of its features highlights the distinctiveness of the magazine's audience, a decidedly bicultural and bilingual uniqueness that could not be captured without the codeswitches. The examples here are from *Latina*, March 1999, April and May 2000, and November 2014.

(36) *Flacas*, beware! *Mujeres con curvas* have a lot to offer.
Skinnies women with curves _____.
'Skinny women beware! Women with curves (curvy women) have a lot to offer.'

(37) Want to be a *millonaria*?
_____ millionaire
Want to be a millionaire?

(38) *Y tú, m'ija*, it's time you realize he doesn't really make you happy.
And you, my daughter, _____
_____
'And you, my daughter, it's time you realize he doesn't really make you happy.'

(39) And a spirit as vibrant as the *colores* of a *piñata*.
_____ colors ___ piñata
'And a spirit as vibrant as the colors of a piñata.'

(40) *Gracias a Dios*, it's Friday.
thanks to God, _____
'Thank God, it's Friday.'

(41) Your *novio* is pushing 30 and still living with his mom.
___ boyfriend _____.
'Your boyfriend is pushing 30 and still living with his mom.'

Analyzing the mix of Spanish and English in *Latina* nearly 20 years ago, I concluded that the codeswitching in *Latina*, taken as a whole, was a new discourse norm that identified the users as members of a community who shared common experiences as immigrants and their descendants, bound together through heritage and culture. As the examples (36)–(41) show, none of the switches into Spanish are linguistically necessary—all the words exist in English. Consequently, we need to consider a different purpose for the codeswitches. I determined that intentional codeswitching was used to create a sense of belonging and solidarity for its targeted readership. The acceptance of Spanglish in this venue was in fact signaling and indexing a shift in the status of the Latinx community in the US, acknowledging the presence of a minority speech community in a glossy lifestyle magazine, sold side by side with other lifestyle publications such as *Vogue*, *GQ*, and *Cosmopolitan*. It is especially significant that Spanglish appears and is highlighted in a national publication that features Latinx celebrities from Associate Justice of the Supreme Court Sonia Maria Sotomayor to Jennifer Lopez and Bruno Mars. It's noteworthy that as the Latinx influence has grown nationally on the political front, Spanish codeswitches are used less frequently in *Latina*, but the focus on the Latina identity remains core to the publication.

The overall takeaway is that codeswitching has become a recognizable, meaningful language choice and mixed-language discourse as a hybrid language variety may be intentionally used to underscore and challenge prevailing social power dynamics and imbalances. It can also signal a shift in the existing social order and delineate ideological, political, social, and cultural territory as well as establish a bilingual/bicultural community's voice in the larger community. The photograph in Figure 3.1 shows a banner in front of the Immaculate Conception Roman Catholic Church in a diverse neighborhood in Chicago. Twenty-nine percent of Chicago's population is Hispanic and the church borders a predominantly Hispanic neighborhood. Notice the codeswitches in the first two phrases. Here the codeswitching is directed toward the bilingual Spanish-English community, likely the second or third generation. It gives an approving nod to both the blended cultures and blended languages common in the neighborhood.

Figure 3.1 Bilingual church banner, Bridgeport neighborhood in Chicago.

(42) KEEP <u>TRANQUILO</u> AND PRAY IN SPANGLISH
_____ calm _____
'Keep calm and pray in Spanglish'
(43) Join us every <u>sábado</u>
_____ Saturday
'Join us every Saturday'

The ubiquitousness of codeswitching and its acceptance as part of everyday life and discourse is further supported by its use in programs depicting immigrant families and their descendants such as *Jane the Virgin* (Latinx family) and *Fresh off the Boat* (Taiwanese-American family) on commercial television, and in film. In the first few minutes of the movie *Crazy Rich Asians* there is a flurry of texts in English, Malay, Chinese, and Singlish, from New York to Singapore, as everyone tries to figure out who Rachel Chu is and why the handsome catch-of-the-century, Nick, is dating her. One text reads: "<u>Wah</u>! So many Rachel Chus, <u>lah</u>!" The underlined words *wah* and *lah* are Singlish. Another texter responds with "Alamak!"

Thinking Matters

Look up Singlish, also known as Singapore English. Find out which languages come together to produce Singlish and who speaks it. Then look up the discourse particles *wah*, *lah*, and *alamak* to find out what they mean. How many uses does *lah* have?

In her review of *Crazy Rich Asians*, Stephanie Foo highlights the two previous examples and writes of her emotional reaction to the use of Singlish, "That was it—I heard people talking like they had in my house growing up, and … waterworks" (www.vox.com/first-person /2018/8/8/17662164/crazy-rich-asians-movie-premiere).

As we shall see, the emotional bond between language and identity is layered, a bond that has been employed in literature as well as in advertising and signage to connect with and draw in readers and consumers.

3.5 Codeswitching in Literature and Public Domains

Thinking Matters

In a recent television advertisement for a Mexican beer, the commercial ends with the written words "Keep it interesante". Another commercial from a fast food chain asks us to "Enjoy mas". What is the function of codeswitching in these national television ads?

Although codeswitching in writing is not a new phenomenon, as an area of study it hasn't received the attention it deserves. As with the purposeful use of codeswitching in *Latina*, we can agree that using multiple languages in fiction is also purposeful. Authors have used multiple languages and dialects as a storytelling device for centuries, though not always for the same reasons. Some have deployed codeswitching strategically to bring authenticity and texture to narratives and dialogs, as in classics such as *The Adventures of Huckleberry Finn*. For others it is a political device to bring attention to minority voices and ethnic identities, to evoke emotions, and/or to portray the reality of living a bicultural life. In the last two decades, we've witnessed a steady growth in the use of multiple languages and dialects in the multicultural literature genre. From short stories to novels to performance pieces, codeswitching is used to help tell stories of lives at crossroads of languages and cultures. The juxtapositioning of languages gives voice to bilingual readers' experience, while inviting monolingual readers to join or at least get a closer look at the other communities that coexist with their own.[5] Examples of multilingual literature range from the Chicano experience in Chicago in the 1980s in Sandra Cisneros's *House on Mango Street*, to Junot Diaz's short stories and novels (e.g., *Drown*, *The Brief and Wondrous Life of Oscar Wao*), Khaled Hosseini's Afghani protagonist in the *Kite Runner*, Mikael Niemi's novel *Popular Music*, theater and performance art pieces by Luis Valdez (e.g., *Zoot Suit*), and work by Guillermo Gómez-Peña (e.g., *Warriors for Gringostroika*). In some cases, typical of older literature, codeswitching is a way for authors to elevate their own profile as intellectuals. For instance, Puhr (2017, p. 2) suggests that Nabokov used multiple languages in three of his novels (*Lolita*, *Pnin*, and *King, Queen, Knave*) to show his superiority as a writer "who is not bound by to any particular nation or language".

Essentially, codeswitching in mainstream publications reveals traits of the social power dynamic between the majority and the minority speech communities, each represented through their language choice. Intentional mixed code can delineate territory, socially and politically, and flips the balance of power in favor of the minority speech community: within the mixed-code medium, the bilingual community is the insider and the monolingual community is the outsider. Ultimately, in all of these instances, we witness the meta-linguistic force of intentional code choice, beyond the actual words. Each chosen language is meant to deliver additional culturally significant information to the reader, whether it is to help situate the reader in the physical context of the tale, to highlight readers' isolation from or connection to a community, or to tell us more about the author.

Thinking Matters

We can find codeswitching in tweets, blogs, and other computer-mediated communication (CMC). What purpose or function do you think codeswitching serves in these venues? If you are a bilingual, have you ever codeswitched when tweeting, emailing, or engaged in other CMC?

3.6 Linguistic Landscapes: Language Choice & Multiple Codes in Public Spaces

What does it mean when languages other than a community's dominant language are used in public domains such as on street signs, storefronts, and advertisements? (see Figure 3.2). Living in multilingual, multicultural societies, many of us have become accustomed to seeing street signs, store signs, billboards and other public signs in multiple languages. Whether walking down streets in Chicago neighborhoods, Los Angeles, Berlin, Tokyo, Nairobi, or Isfahan, across the globe we can see multilingual signs in many neighborhoods, a reflection of the ethnic groups who have made their homes in these neighborhoods. Most

Figure 3.2 Café menu sidewalk sign, in English and Persian. Isfahan, Iran.

of us don't give this rich landscape of languages and cultures a second thought. However, in their study of the languages used on signs in public spaces in Canada, Landry and Bourhis (1997) did just that. In their study, they coined the term 'Linguistic Landscapes', which they defined as "the visibility and salience of languages on public and commercial signs in a given territory or region" (p. 23). Their focus was on the languages used on public and commercial signs in various ethnic minority neighborhoods. They hypothesized that when signs were in the community's languages they revealed the power relationship and status of the communities relative to the majority language and population, and to each other. Moreover, Landry and Bourhis proposed that when signs were in the community language, they served to reinforce the community's ethnic and linguistic identity. Their research concludes that multilingual signs could serve two functions: an informational function, such as street and road signs and signs on government buildings, or a symbolic function to mark ethnic territory and valorize the community language, thus bolstering community members' sense of belonging and their community's vitality. Thus, multilingual signage also helps to make visible the sometimes-invisible minority communities that work and thrive in these neighborhoods. Multilingual signs also have the well-known practical marketing function of reaching the widest audience.

In a recent comprehensive study of signage used in the Julfa district in Isfahan, Iran, Saeed Rezaei and Maedeh Tadayyon (2018) found the languages used on the many storefronts and street signs of this trendy area revealed much about the identity and identification of the predominantly Armenian Christian residents of this district. With its numerous UNESCO-protected historic sites, Isfahan is a travel destination for international tourists as well as for visitors from all over Iran. Isfahan, and in particular the Julfa district of Isfahan, is a long-time home to Armenian Christians. With a representative in the Iranian parliament, Armenians are a small but strong minority in Iran, who practice their own religion, speak their own language (in addition to Persian) and follow their own cultural practices. Though much of the signage Rezaei and Tadayyon found is multilingual (Persian, English, Armenian), of the 323 signs they photographed throughout the Julfa area, the Armenian language was used in only 39. Persian was used in 278 signs and English in 212 signs.

Figure 3.3 Storefront, Julfa district, Isfahan.

Figure 3.4 Museum sign, Julfa district, Isfahan.

Through their documenting of signage, Rezaei and Tadayyon arrive at a noteworthy conclusion. They see the signs as a reflection of the nature of the Armenian identity interwoven with their Christian and Iranian identities, on the one hand, and the exoticism of the Armenian speech community and culture for Iranians and international tourists on the other. Moreover, the linguistic landscape of the Julfa district reveals and reinforces an interesting balance between three linguistic realities: English as a global language, Persian as a ubiquitous national language, and Armenian as a local language of a strong and undeniable minority presence. In the shop window in Figure 3.3, we see signs in all three languages. Here the intent is primarily to inform Iranians, despite the Marlboro sign. In Figure 3.4, we see a sign for the museum in Armenian, Persian, and English. Including Armenian in the sign serves two functions: to reaffirm the Armenian identity of the district, and to inform national and international visitors. The photos in Figures 3.3 and 3.4 were taken and shared by the authors, Saeed Rezaei and Maedeh Tadayyon.

In Chapter 2 we noted the use of English to advertise products in places where English is not the community language because English brings with it the image of cool, Western, modern, and exciting youthfulness. Thus, the language used in public spaces as part of commercial signage may serve to project a desired association and should not be mistaken as a reflection of an existing language community (Gorter, 2013).

Others have made similar observations. For example, in discussing the linguistic landscape of Berlin, Germany, Fuller (forthcoming) notes: "While in some instances English indexes Anglophone cultures, in the majority of the cases English is used to construct a global image for the business and consumer". Additionally, from her study of Turkish language signage in Berlin, Fuller concludes that the use of Turkish has two functions. In the case of shop signs, the use of Turkish signals authenticity, while in predominantly Turkish neighborhoods where the information is already available in German, the use of Turkish is meant to reinforce an "outsider" ideology, which assumes Turkish immigrants and their descendants have either chosen not to be or have not been integrated into German society. As already mentioned, Rezaie and Tadayyon found the same to be true for the use of English in the signs they encountered in the Julfa, Isfahan, district.

3.6.1 Translanguaging

Translanguaging theory is another approach to multilingualism. Colin Baker, Ofelia Garcia, and Li Wei, among a few others, have opened a new window through which to look at multilingualism. Rooted in bilingual education and pedagogy, translanguaging theory opposes making distinctions among languages and calls for a perspective that sees speakers' multiple languages as part of a unitary system. Vogel and Garcia (2017, p. 1) explain:

> The theory posits that rather than possessing two or more autonomous language systems, as has been traditionally thought, bilinguals, multilinguals, and indeed, all users of language, select and deploy particular features from a unitary linguistic repertoire to make meaning and to negotiate particular communicative contexts. Translanguaging also represents an approach to language pedagogy that affirms and leverages students' diverse and dynamic language practices in teaching and learning.

As you can imagine, the translanguaging theory of bilingualism is controversial, as it proposes to dismantle much of the research and findings of the last 70 years, not to mention the centuries of descriptive and comparative language studies and documents. The strength of this proposal, though, is in the fact that it highlights a facet of bilingualism that is specifically relevant to education—that of looking at bilingualism as a resource for speakers, one that should be embraced and worked into the curriculum. Proponents of translanguaging theory reiterate, as many other scholars have, that bilingualism is more than just knowledge of and access to two or more linguistic systems and that language is a resource for bilinguals. Additionally, they highlight the sociocultural and contextual aspects of bilingualism *during* communication, and in particular within the context of young school-age bilinguals' education. Ostensibly, they are moved by issues of social justice and the need to eradicate the injustices arising when language is used as a means to marginalize speakers of minority languages. However, their main psycholinguistic premise that the bilingual draws from a single store of language is not borne out at this time. In fact there is psycholinguistic evidence from language experiments with bilingual children and adults that strengthens a separate-systems hypothesis where the bilinguals' languages appear to be operating as independent rule-governed systems (e.g., Kovelman, Baker, & Petitto, 2008; Ma, Hu, Xi, Shen, Ge, Geng, Wu, Guo, & Yao, 2014; Zhang, Wang, Huang, Li, Qiu, Shen, & Xie, 2015; Mahootian & Schott, 2017). We will discuss these and other relevant research studies in Chapter 5. For now, translanguaging remains a new approach which will benefit from more research by linguists, psycholinguists, and educators.

3.7 Attitudes Toward Codeswitching

Codeswitching. Virtually all bilinguals do it. Even when they say they don't. Codeswitching is a natural by-product of bilingualism, or more precisely, a way to use language which bilinguals, regardless of language, gender, age, or socioeconomic class, have access to and employ. In fact, the practice of codeswitching is so common that many bilingual speech communities have named the mixed variety they use: for example, Chinglish is a mix of Chinese and English, and Spanish and English combine to produce Spanglish—probably the most well known and controversial of code-mixed language in the United States. We also have Poglish (Polish and English), Perglish (Persian and English), and Frenglish (French and English), to name just a few other pairings. So why deny the ability to manage multiple grammars and create code-mixed utterances that other bilinguals of the same speech community readily understand? Despite clear evidence that code-mixed utterances are grammatical constructions and not just a hodge-podge of languages, and that they serve various discourse functions, in many communities codeswitching has a stigmatized status. This is not to say that all bilinguals or all bilingual communities consider codeswitching to be negative. In fact, throughout bilingual and monolingual communities, depending on the languages involved, and the class, age, education, profession, etc., of the speakers, one finds that attitudes toward mixed language use range from positive to negative.

Though we can't precisely predict attitudes across various bilingual communities and individuals, we do see a pattern. For example, older generations, who are often the initial immigrants, and newly arrived immigrants typically have a negative response to code switching, especially when their cultural norms and values are in conflict with those of their host nation. They misidentify codeswitching as a loss of pride for the home culture, a sign of disrespect to the community elders, and/or a lack of mastery of one or both of their languages. Accusations of laziness and ignorance are heaped on top of all that. They avoid codeswitching themselves and expect the languages to be kept separate, and hence 'pure.' Ultimately they are afraid that losing any part of their language means losing their connection to the home, family, and friends they left behind, and their identity. As we discussed earlier, for many, the language they grew up with is an inextricable part of their identity; therefore, losing command of the language is equated with a loss of identity. For younger generations, the narrative is significantly different: for those who immigrated as children with their families or were born after their parents' immigration, their host nation's language and culture are as much a part of their identity as are their heritage languages and cultures. Even though they may be pressed to avoid codeswitching in the presence of their elders or at any time at home, codeswitching is an added resource in their repertoire and a means of identifying with others who share in their experience and understand their history.

Outside pressures to conform to monolingual standards of speaking one language at a time (without mixing the languages) and negative attitudes toward immigrants from the host nation also add to the negative attitudes toward language mixing within bilingual and monolingual communities. When not accepted by the host country, individuals face increasing pressure to hold on to all aspects of their heritage, including language, and thereby maintain a sense of belonging to a community (in this case the community they left behind). A case in point is the plight of Mexican-Americans. Until recently, Mexican-Americans have had to struggle for a position in American society. Romaine (1995) notes that until the mid-1990s, among Mexican-Americans, codeswitching was highly stigmatized and referred to pejoratively. She points to the reversal of the previously derogatory use of *pocho*[6] in California and the southwestern United States to refer to the variety of mixed code Spanish-English spoken by Chicanos[7]. She ties this positive shift to a heightened ethnic awareness among Chicanos/as and their increased socioeconomic status. In other words, by establishing an identity in the host country, successive generations more readily embrace their bicultural and/or bilingual identities. Still, many Spanish-English bilinguals in the United States think of Spanglish as 'slang' or 'street talk', instead of a casual speech style, even while they use it with family and friends as part of everyday conversations. However, the mix of the same two languages, Spanish and English, in some ethnic communities, is considered a norm and, in fact, has an additive value. For example, Puerto Rican Spanish-English bilinguals in New York have long held a positive attitude toward codeswitching; mixing the two languages is an important way to show speakers' affiliation and connection to both of their cultures and to one another.

Fuller (2012) conducted an interesting study that (i) highlights the multiple variables that can influence the use of mixed code and switching between languages, and (ii) underscores the relationship between language choice and identity. She compared the use of bilingual discourse in two bilingual programs in two different settings: a Spanish-English classroom in southern Illinois in the US and a German-English classroom in Berlin, Germany. Surprisingly, she found that in the German-English program, children were careful to keep their two languages 'pure' by not mixing or switching between the two languages. The children in the Spanish-English program, however, used much more, and more complex, bilingual discourse. Fuller's interpretation of these results is that the children in the German-English bilingual program, as participants in elite bilingualism, had more to lose; keeping German and English separate from each other provided them with cultural capital that they could lose if they did not keep with the language purism ideology. The children in the Spanish-English classroom were immigrant bilinguals, a stigmatized status, and thus they had little to lose; so at least in the context of their classroom, where bilingualism was valued, they used both languages and codeswitched to construct their identities as peers and students.

Over the last four decades, results from studies across bilingual communities in various countries have arrived at similar conclusions—a mix of positive and negative attitudes toward codeswitching. For example, in a study of codeswitching by Greek Cypriots in London, Gardner-Chloros, McEntee-Atalianis, and Finnis (2005) found both favorable and unfavorable attitudes toward switching. Positive and negative attitudes by Cypriots were stratified based on participants' occupation, education, socioeconomic class, and age. For example, younger respondents and respondents from lower socioeconomic classes held more positive attitudes toward codeswitching than did older respondents and those who were more educated. Additionally, younger respondents regarded codeswitching as an advantage, providing them with yet another speech variety to connect with others. Gardner-Chloros et al. concluded that codeswitching was becoming more acceptable in the Greek Cypriot community in London.

Dewaele and Wei (2014) obtained some similar results from their survey of attitudes toward codeswitching in which 36 monolinguals and 2,034 bi/multilinguals participated. The participants were from 204 nationalities and included 1,535 women and 428 men (107 participants did not provide gender information). The mean age of the participants was 34.6. The majority of participants were from Western nations where there was significant ethnic diversity. The largest group of participants was Americans, followed by British, Dutch, Belgians, and Germans.[8] The first language of the majority was English, followed by Dutch, French, Spanish, and German. The majority second languages were English (881 speakers), followed by French, Spanish, and German. Education levels ranged from high school diplomas, the smallest group, to secondary degrees (BAs, MAs, PhDs).

Overall, Dewaele and Wei found that attitudes toward codeswitching were "linked to personality, language learning history and current linguistic practices, as well as some sociobiographical variables" (p. 235). Specifically, they discovered that the participants who were the most proficient and those who were the least proficient in their languages had more positive attitudes than those with mid-level proficiency. Their findings also showed that speakers who had more contact with diverse multilingual environments, growing up in multilingual homes and working in ethnically diverse settings, had "significantly more positive attitudes toward CS". Furthermore, they found correlations between gender and attitudes and education and attitudes: females and participants with the most and the least education had more positive attitudes toward codeswitching than did males and participants with mid-range education levels, respectively. Somewhat surprisingly, in contrast to some of the other studies mentioned, their results also showed that younger participants (those in their teens and early twenties) were less approving of codeswitching than their older participants were.

Thinking Matters

Can you think of any reasons why younger speakers in the Dewaele and Wei study were less approving of codeswitching than the older participants?

On the whole, from these and other studies, we see that outcomes may differ across bilingual communities, but the variables that influence whether bilinguals will embrace or reject codeswitching within their communities are the same, with age, education, occupation, and gender topping the list.

3.8 Mechanisms: The Rules of Codeswitching

Most of the initial linguistic research on bilingualism revolved around social and functional questions. As for grammatical analysis, some researchers simply wrote off codeswitching as an ad hoc, anything-goes mish-mash of languages. By the mid-1970s, however, a number of linguists began to think about the grammar of codeswitched utterances and what rules, if any, governed the mixed utterances produced by bilinguals of a variety of language pairs. Since then, much has been written, and many models have been proposed to explain how two or more grammatical systems come together to form a single phrase or sentence. These models have sought to address three main questions:

1. Are codeswitched sentences grammatical?
2. Is it possible to mix any two languages or must both languages have the same word order? For example can English, which is a *Subject-Verb-Object* language (e.g., *Leila bought cookies*), mix with Japanese or Persian, both of which are *Subject-Object-Verb* languages (e.g., the Persian sentence, *Leila shirini* [cookies] *kharid* [bought])?
3. Does the combination of each pair of languages create a third grammar?

The answer to the first question is an unequivocal and resounding 'yes'. Codeswitching is a natural, rule-governed use of language, and the resulting mixed-language utterances are grammatical. Along the way to answering the remaining two questions about the rules governing codeswitching, four main approaches developed:

- Descriptive approaches
- Approaches involving a third grammar specific to codeswitching
- Approaches with special rules for codeswitching, but no third grammar
- Approaches without special rules or third grammars

Descriptive approaches got the ball rolling by simply describing the product of codeswitching in terms of the word categories that appeared in mixed sentences (e.g., nouns, verbs, adjectives), and where in an utterance they occurred (e.g., subject, object, prepositional phrase). For example, since they did not find the types of switches shown in (44) and (45) in their Spanish-English data (where the subject pronoun is in one language and the verb is in the other), Timm (1975) and Gumperz (1976) proposed that switching could not occur between the subject pronoun and the verb that has tense.

(44) <u>Ella</u> left. (45) She <u>se fue.</u>
    she   left
    'She left.' 'She left.'

However, such switches do occur, as we saw earlier in the Arabic-English example in (9), repeated in (46) for convenience. Here the pronoun 'you' is in Arabic *inta* and the verb is in English.

(46) inta hang-<u>ha</u> up
    You   -it
    'you hang it up' (Ar-Eng, Mohammed, 1983)

Others proposed that switches couldn't occur between adjectives and nouns unless both languages had the same adjective placement. Accordingly, we should not find codeswitches in natural speech such as the one here. In (47) we see a switch between the English adjective *red* and the Persian noun *shamduni* ('geranium'). However, English and Persian have different orders for nouns and adjectives. In English the adjectives comes <u>before</u> the noun, but in Persian the adjective comes <u>after</u> the noun.

(47) I'm planting red <u>shamduni</u> this time.
     _____ geranium(s)_____
     'I'm planting red <u>geraniums</u> this time.' (Eng-Pers)

Though these early studies were correct in their descriptions of the data, the descriptions were limited to the examples they had collected and to the two languages, Spanish and English, with which they were working.

Rules and third grammars—The next wave of models included a series of codeswitching-specific rules which were intended to predict where in a sentence bilinguals would and would not switch. The first in this series of approaches to codeswitching was Sankoff and Poplack's (1981) three-grammar approach. They proposed that bilinguals have a separate codeswitching grammar in addition to the monolingual grammars of each of their two languages. Like Timm, Pfaff, and Gumperz, they also examined switches produced by Spanish-English bilinguals. Sankoff and Poplack envisioned a codeswitching grammar that would combine the lexicon and rules of each of the monolingual grammars. For example, in the case of Spanish-English, bilinguals would possess three grammatical systems:

- Lexicon and Grammar of English
- Lexicon and Grammar of Spanish
- Lexicons and Grammars of English and Spanish combined to form a single grammatical system

Additionally, they proposed two rules (constraints) for codeswitching. The first rule, the Free Morpheme Constraint, predicts speakers would not combine the words of one language with affixes of another language. This means that we would not hear speakers producing utterances like those in examples (48) and (49). However, they do. In (48) the English word 'park' combines with the Spanish suffix *--iendo* (equivalent to the English progressive ending '–ing') to produce *park-iendo*. In (56) the Persian suffix *–et* ('your') is attached to the English noun *lawyer*.

(48) park-<u>iendo</u> (Sp-Eng)
     -ing
  'parking'

(49) Lawyer-<u>et</u> will tell you what to do. (Eng-Pers)
  _____-your _____
  'Your lawyer will tell you what to do.'

Their second rule, the Equivalence Constraint, proposes that switches are only possible when the order of words in phrases and the order of phrases in sentences are the same in both languages. For example, the Equivalence Constraint predicts that there will be no switches between English and Japanese because Japanese word order and English word order are significantly different from each other. In Japanese, the verb comes at the end of the sentence, whereas in English the verb comes immediately after the subject. Therefore, according to the Equivalence Constraint, bilingual Japanese-English speakers won't produce switches between verbs and objects.

However, in example (50) we can see that Japanese-English speakers *do* make such combinations (Kumar, 2013, p. 43); here, the English verb *are* is followed by the Japanese phrase *eigo no sensei* ('English teacher').

(50) You made a mistake!! You are <u>eigo no sensei</u>!
    You made a mistake!! You are English of teacher
    'You made a mistake!! You are an English teacher!'

Likewise, in the English-Persian example in (51), we see a switch between an English object and a Persian verb. Like Japanese and unlike English, the object in Persian goes before the verb. In this conversation, the speaker is telling her friends about an incident in which a customer gave her ten dollars for an item that cost twenty dollars. She switches between the English object 'ten dollars' and the Persian verb *dad* ('gave'), to produce the sentence *ten dollars dad*.

(51) ten dollars <u>dad</u>
    Object   Verb
    _____ <u>gave</u>
    '(she) <u>gave</u> ten dollars' (Mahootian, 1993)

In addition to the limitations of the of their codeswitching rules, a number of researchers also criticized the notion of a third codeswitching grammar on conceptual grounds. Recall that in the three-grammar model, for every two languages, a third code-mixed grammar is required. This means that a trilingual speaker would be managing seven grammars and that a quadrilingual speaker must juggle 15 grammars. Add another language, and the speaker who knows five languages would require a very large number of grammars to be in play and at the ready. From a language processing perspective, such an increase in the number of grammars seems highly unlikely because the speaker would presumably have to use some extra amount of mental energy to keep the other grammars from interfering when only one, or a few, are in use. For a more detailed discussion of storing and using multiple grammars, see Chapter 5.

Approaches with special rules for codeswitching, but no third grammar—Over the next few years, as more data was gathered, it became clear that the constraints on codeswitching proposed earlier did not apply to most language pairs. Other constrained-based models followed, each suggesting additional codeswitching-specific rules and predicting that certain types of switches would or wouldn't occur in the speech of bilinguals.[9] For example, some proposed that there would be no switches between articles and nouns or between prepositions and their objects. However, these theories also turned out to make incorrect predictions. Data collected from natural speech across a variety of language pairs shows counterexamples to the various proposed constraints.

Examples (52) and (53) show switches between articles and nouns in English-Spanish and Irish-English sentences, respectively:

(52) The color of the <u>tapete</u> is red.
        _____ rug ____
    'The color of the rug is red.' (Eng-Sp)
(53) Beidh an <u>jackpot</u> anocht a'ainn.
    Will be the _____ tonight do
    'We'll get the jackpot tonight.' (Ir-Eng, Laoire, 2016)

In example (54) we see a switch between a French preposition *à* ('to') and its indirect object Michigan Avenue.

(54) Tu peux aller à <u>Michigan Avenue</u>.
   You can go to _____
   'You can go to Michigan Avenue.' (Fr-Eng)

Approaches without special rules or third grammars—In the early 1990s a few researchers set out to develop more comprehensive accounts of the grammar of codeswitching. From their efforts, two new models emerged. In 1993, based on data from 12 language pairs, including languages which did not share word orders, I proposed dispensing with codeswitching-specific rules and third grammars, and instead approached codeswitching as a natural language process rather than one that required extra rules or additional grammars. I proposed that the same grammatical rules which apply to the bilingual's individual monolingual grammars apply as a team to produce mixed code utterances. Hence, no additional rules or grammars are required. Consequently, I offered a model based on a fundamental grammatical relationship within phrases and sentences that exists in all languages, the Head-Complement Principle (HCP) model of codeswitching.[10] The HCP spells out which elements of phrases are open to being switched and replaced by elements from another language (**complements**) and which are not (**heads**).

Heads and complements are part of the grammar of every language and language variety, a universal principle of language. This simple principle is used to predict where switches can occur in any given phrase or sentence, regardless of the languages involved. For example, in the phrase *the underworld*, the article *the* is the **head** and the noun *underworld* is the **complement**. In the prepositional phrase *in the basement*, the preposition *in* is the **head** of the prepositional phrase and *the basement* is the **complement** of the phrase. The same types of head-complement relationships hold in other languages, regardless of word order differences. For instance, Japanese uses postpositions instead of prepositions to form phrases such as *in the basement*. Postpositions follow their complements, thus producing the Japanese phrase in (55) where *chika* ('basement') is followed by the postposition *de* ('in'):

(55) *chika de*
   basement in
   'in the basement'

Now let's consider a codeswitch between English and Japanese. The HCP predicts that for a phrase such as *in the basement*, a Japanese-English speaker could either say the phrase in (56) or the one in (57). (Note: Japanese does not use articles such as 'the'):

(56) **in** <u>chika</u>
(57) basement **<u>de</u>**

In both sentences, the complements are switched ('chika in (56) and 'basement' in (57)). The heads keep their original positions according to the language of the head (English 'in' comes before the complement, Japanese 'de' comes after the complement)

Naturally occurring date corroborates these predictions, as shown in example (58) from Nishimura (1985).

(58) I slept with her basement <u>de</u>.

<u>   </u>
in

'I slept with her in the basement'

So far, the HCP has accurately predicted the variety of switches found in natural bilingual discourse that were not predicted by previous models. The HCP's predictions hold for all language pairs, even those that have different word orders from each other (e.g., Japanese and English). The HCP model has proved to be a fruitful approach to understanding how bilinguals combine two or more languages and produce grammatical utterances. It remains a robust framework for addressing codeswitching and has attracted the attention of other researchers, some of whom have used the same principles and framework recast in different terminology.[11]

Another model that has moved away from specialized codeswitching rules and additional codeswitching grammars is Carol Myers-Scotton's Matrix Language Frame model (1993, 2002). The MLF model distinguishes between two types of morphemes to explain how codeswitched sentences are grammatical and rule-governed. The model relies on identifying a matrix language, the main foundation language of the codeswitch, and an embedded language. The MLF model also works from a set of universal language principles to distinguish between different types of morphemes during codeswitching.[12]

Overall, the principle-based approaches, which avoid constraints and extra codeswitching grammars, have proved to deliver the most comprehensive accounts for codeswitching across many language pairs. These approaches, together with early investigations into bilingualism, show the progression of research spanning from a view of codeswitching as a dynamic social phenomenon to codeswitching as a language phenomenon that can inform linguistic theory at structural levels of syntax and morphology, and as we will see, provide insights into language acquisition and other cognitive processes.

3.9 Summary

In this chapter, we discovered how and why bilinguals may at times combine their two languages, intentionally or unintentionally, when speaking or writing, to produce grammatical discourse. We also learned that codeswitching may be driven by cultural expectations, and that attitudes toward codeswitching can differ from one multilingual community to another, across age, gender, education, and occupation.

Discussion Questions and Projects

1. Read *The Pura Principle* (www.newyorker.com/magazine/2010/03/22/the-pura-principle) by Junot Diaz. Why do you think Diaz uses codeswitching in this story? How does it affect the story? How does it affect you as the reader?
2. In your opinion, when emojis are used in texting, emails, and other messaging platforms, can it be considered codeswitching? Explain your answer.
3. Find five willing participants and ask them to write a definition for identity. Next, ask them to write a few sentences about their own identity. Did you find any similarities across the five definitions? How about across the five self-descriptions?
4. Choose one of the articles listed in the references to read and then summarize in two pages. Your summary should include major question(s), method(s) used, subject population, any special equipment used to collect data, results, and conclusions.
5. Interview a bilingual: find someone who is bilingual and uses two languages regularly at work and/or home and/or with friends.

Use these interview questions to find out about his or her languages and language use. Feel free to add your own questions as well.

Bilingualism and Codeswitching Interview

Ask your participant the following questions:

1. What languages do you speak?
2. How long have you been speaking each language?
3. Who do you speak each language with?
4. When do you speak each language?
5. What topics do you talk about in each language?
6. Do you ever mix the two languages together? If yes, when do you mix them?
7. Who do you codeswitch with? (*To the interviewer*: explain to the interviewee what the term 'codeswitch' means.)
8. How does your bilingual community feel about codeswitching?
9. How do you feel about codeswitching?
10. Ask your participant to provide three examples which contain codeswitching.
11. Go through the codeswitching examples presented in this chapter to see whether they follow or contradict the Head-Complement Principle model discussed in Section 3.8. Can you identify the heads and complements in each?

Notes

1 Examples without researcher name were provided by bilingual Linguistics MA students and graduates in my classes from conversations with other bilinguals. My thanks to Heyli Gomez (Spanish-English), Sonya Chen (Chinese-English), Hanadi Elmanaseer (Arabic-English).
2 This example was shared by Heyli Gomez who went on to elaborate on the codeswitch: "I think this is due to the fact that her husband is most comfortable in Spanish. He learned English as an adult, so although he knows how to speak English, he mostly speaks Spanish."
3 As reported in the *New York Times*, December 5, 2018: "Speaking at a technology conference on Tuesday, Ms. Merkel, known as a staid, no-drama politician, told a self-deprecating anecdote about being widely mocked online five years ago after she described the internet as some mysterious expanse

of 'uncharted territory.' She chuckled at the memory of the digital blow-back. 'It generated quite a shitstorm,' she said, using the English term — because Germans, it turns out, do not have one of their own." For the full article, go to https://www.nytimes.com/2018/12/05/world/europe/merkel-storm-translation-germany.html.

4   Blavity is an internet media company and website, created by and for black millennials. Their mission is to "economically and creatively support Black millennials across the African diaspora, so they can pursue the work they love, and change the world in the process". (https://blavity.com/).

5   For further discussion of language mixing in writing, and analysis of the codeswitching in Khaled Hosseini's *Kite Runner*, Luiz Vadez's *Zoot Suit*, and Gómez-Peña *Warriors for Gringostroika*, see Sebba, M., Mahootian, S., and Jonsson, C. (Eds.) (2012), *Language mixing and codeswitching: Approaches to mixed language written discourse*.

6   Pocho refers to Americanized Mexicans, or Mexicans who have lost their culture. Here, culture largely means the Spanish language. Until recently, among Mexican-Americans, pocho has been considered derogatory, an accusation hurled at someone believed to be acting white, too Americanized. In recent years, the term has been appropriated and mostly embraced by Chicanos as an in-group term of camaraderie. Take a minute and learn some Mexican slang from Mexican-American Salma Hayek: www.pocho.com/vocab-101-mexican-slang-with-profe-salma-hayek-video/.

7   Chicano/a is interchangeable with Mexican-American and often preferred by Mexican-Americans in the Southwest and western United States.

8   Participants included Canadians, Poles, French, Spaniards, Chinese, Croatians, Turks, Swiss, Portuguese, Swedes, Italians, and Japanese, each of which had more than 25 participants, and finally, representatives of 187 other nationalities with fewer than 25 participants each.

9   Bentahila and Davies (1983), Woolford (1983), Joshi (19), DiScuillo, Muysken, and Singh (1986) among others, proposed various constraints for how they believed codeswitching worked grammatically. For a comprehensive review of the various proposed codeswitching constraints, see Mahootian, S. (2006), Codeswitching and Mixing. *Encyclopedia of Language & Linguistics* (2006), vol. 2, 511–527.

10 The Head-Complement Principle (HCP) states that heads determine the syntactic properties of their complements in codeswitching and monolingual contexts alike: heads determine the phrase structure position, syntactic category, and feature content of their arguments. More detailed discussions of the HCP model can be found in Mahootian (1996) and Mahootian and Santorini (1996).

11 An additional strength of this approach is that it can accommodate any generative syntactic platform, whether Chomskyan minimalism or lexically based models (such as the Tree-adjoining Grammar model used by Mahootian, 1993). See MacSwan, J. (1999). *A Minimalist Approach to Intrasentential Code Switching*. New York: Garland Press, for a recasting of the HCP using a minimalist framework.

12 The complexities of the MLF model are beyond the scope of this volume. Please check out the references for further readings on this approach.

References and Recommended Readings

Arthur, C. (2017). The cost of codeswitching. TEDx talk. www.youtube.com/watch?v=Bo3hRq2RnNI.

Auer, P. (1984). On the meaning of conversational codeswitching. In: P. Auer, & A. do Luizo (Eds.), *Interpretive Sociolinguistics: Migrants, Children, Migrant Children* (pp. 87–112). Tübingen, Germany: Gunter Narr Verlag.

Auer, P., & Dirim, İ. (2003). Socio-cultural orientation, urban youth styles and the spontaneous acquisition of Turkish by non-Turkish adolescents in Germany. In: J.K. Androutsopoulos, & A. Georgakopoulou (Eds.), *Discourse Constructions of Youth Identities. Pragmatics & Beyond New Series 110* (pp. 223–246). Amsterdam, The Netherlands: John Benjamins Publishers.

Bentahila, A. (1983). *Language Attitudes among Arabic-French Bilinguals in Morocco*. Clevedon, UK: Multilingual Matters.

Bentahila, A., & Davies E E (1983). The syntax of Arabic-French code-switching. *Lingua*, 59, 301–330.

Blommaert, J. (2005). *Discourse*. Cambridge, UK: Cambridge University Press.

Bullock, S. (2014). Language Ideologies in Morocco. Anthropology Department Honors Papers. 11. http://digitalcommons.conncoll.edu/anthrohp/11.

Chana, U., & Romaine, S. (1984). Evaluative Reactions to Punjabi/English Code-switching. *Journal of Multilingual and Multicultural Development*. 5(6): 447–473. doi: 10.1080/01434632.1984.9994174.

Cook, V., & Wei, L. (Eds.). (2016). *The Cambridge Handbook of Linguistic Multi-Competence*. Cambridge, UK: Cambridge University Press.

de Fina, A. (2007). Group identity, narrative, and self-representation. In: de Fina, A., Schiffrin, D., & Bamberg, M. (Eds.), *Discourse and Identity* (pp. 351–376). Cambridge, UK: Cambridge University Press.

Dewaele, J., & Wei, L. (2014). Attitudes towards code-switching among adult mono- and multilingual language users. *Journal of Multilingual and Multicultural Development*. 35(3): 235–251. 10.1080/01434632.2013.859687.

Di Sciullo, A., Muysken, P., & Singh, R. (1986). Government and code-mixing. *Linguistics*, 22, 1–24. Edwards, J. (2013). Multilingualism: Some central concepts. In: Bhatia, T., & Ritchie, W. (Eds.), *The Handbook of Bilingualism and Multilingualism*, 2nd edition. Malden, MA: Blackwell Publishers, Ltd.

Edwards, J. (2013). Multilingualism: Some central concepts. In: Bhatia, T., & Ritchie, W. (Eds.), *The Handbook of Bilingualism and Multilingualism*, 2nd edition. Malden, MA: Blackwell Publishers, Ltd.

Eversteijn, N. (2011). All at once: Language choice and codeswitching by Turkish-Dutch teenagers. PhD thesis. Tilburg, the Netherlands: Tilburg University.

Fuller, J.M. (2012). *Bilingual Pre-Teens: Competing Ideologies and Multiple Identities in the US and Germany*. London, UK and New York: Routledge: Taylor and Francis Group.

Gumperz, J.C., & Gumperz, J.J. (1976). The sociolinguistic significance of conversational code-switching. In: J.C. Gumperz, & J.J. Gumperz (Eds.), *Papers on Language and Context: Working Papers no. 46*. Berkeley, CA: Language Behavior Research Laboratory, University of California.

Gumperz, J.J. (1982). *Discourse Strategies: Studies in Interactional Sociolinguistics 1*. Cambridge, UK: Cambridge University Press.

García, O., & Wei, L. (2014). *Translanguaging: Language, Bilingualism and Education*. Basingstoke, UK: Palgrave Macmillan.

Gardner-Chloros, P., McEntee-Atalianis, L.J., & Finnis, K. (2005). Language attitudes and use in a transplanted setting: Greek Cypriots in London. *International Journal of Multilingualism*. 2(1): 52–80. doi: 10.1080/17501220508668376.

Grosjean, F. (1982). *Life with Two Languages*. Cambridge, MA: Harvard University Press.

Jørgensen, J.N. (1998). Children's acquisition of code-switching for power-wielding. In: P. Auer (Ed.), *Codeswitching in Conversation: Language Interaction and Identity* (pp. 237–258). London, UK: Routledge.

Kovelman, I., Baker, S.A., & Petitto, L.A. (2008). Bilingual and monolingual brains compared: A functional magnetic resonance imaging investigation of syntactic processing and a possible "neural signature" of bilingualism. *Journal of Cognitive Neuroscience*. 20(1):153–169. doi: 10.1162/jocn.2008.20011.

Kumar, K. (2013). Code-switching in Japanese and English: A written conversation analysis of a bilingual speaker. *The Journal of Nagasaki University of Foreign Studies*. (17): 37–48.

Landry, R., & Bourhis, R.Y. (1997). Linguistic landscape and ethnolinguistic vitality: An empirical study. *Journal of Language and Social Psychology*. 16(1): 23–49. doi: 10.1177/0261927X970161002.

Laoire, S.N. (2016). Irish-English code-switching: A sociolinguistic perspective. In: Hickey, R. (Ed.), *Sociolinguistics in Ireland* (pp. 81–106). London, UK: Palgrave Macmillan.

Lawson, S., & Sachdev, I. (2000). Codeswitching in Tunisia: Attitudinal and behavioral dimensions. *Journal of Pragmatics*. 32(9): 1343–1361. doi: 10.1016/S0378-2166(99)00103-4.

Luqun, G. (2007). An Investigation on English/Chinese Code-switching in BBS in Chinese Alumni's Community. https://www.era.lib.ed.ac.uk/bitstr eam/1842/1937/1/e-submission.doc.

Ma, H., Hu, J., Xi, J., Shen, W., Ge, J., Geng, F., Wu, Y., Guo, J., & Yao, D. (2014). Bilingual cognitive control in language switching: An fMRI study of English-Chinese late bilinguals. *PLOS ONE*. 9(9): e106468. doi: 10.1371/journal.pone.0106468.

Mahootian S (1993). A null theory of codeswitching. Ph.D. dissertation, Northwestern University.

Mahootian, S. (2005). Linguistic change and social meaning: Codeswitching in the media. *International Journal of Bilingualism*. 9(3–4): 361–375.

Mahootian, S. (2006). Codeswitching and codemixing. In: Brown, K. (Ed.), *The International Encyclopedia of Language and Linguistics*, 2nd edition, Vol. 2 (pp. 511–527). Oxford, UK: Elsevier Ltd.

Mahootian, S. (2012). Resources and repetoires. In: M. Sebba, S. Mahootian, C. Jonsson (Eds.), *Language Mixing and Code-Switching in Writing: Approaches to Mixed-Language Written Discourse* (pp. 192–212). London: Routledge.

Mahootian, S., Kaplan-Weinger, J., Gebhardt, L., & Hallett, R.W. (2017). *Language and Human Behavior: Topics in Linguistics*. Dubuque, IA: Kendall-Hunt Publishers.

Mohamed, F. (1983). Arabic-English Code-switching in the Speech of a Six-Year-Old Child. MS thesis, University of Pennsylvania.

Mahootian, S., & Santorini, B. (1996). Codeswitching and the complement adjunct distinction. *Linguistics Inquiry*. 27(3), 464–479.

Muñoa Barredo, I. (1997). Pragmatic functions of code-switching among Basque-Spanish bilinguals. http://ssl.webs.uvigo.es/actas1997/04/Munhoa. pdf.

Munteanu, D. (2007). Româna vorbită în Spania poate deveni o nouă modalitate lingvistică? *Proceedings of the Conference: Diaspora în Cercetarea Științifică Românească*, Bucharest, Romania.

Myers-Scotton, C. (1993). *Duelling Languages: Grammatical Structure in Codeswitching*. Oxford, UK: Oxford University Press.

Myers-Scotton, C. (2002). *Contact Linguistics: Bilingual Encounters and Grammatical Outcomes*. Oxford, UK: Oxford University Press.

Nishimura, M. (1985). Intrasentential codeswitching in Japanese and English. Ph.D. dissertation, University of Pennsylvania.

Nishimura, M. (1991). Varieties of Japanese/English bilingual speech: Implications for theories of codeswitching and borrowing. Unpublished manuscript, Georgetown University.

Pena, C. (2004). What do bilinguals think about their 'Code-switching'? *RAEL: Revista Electrónica de Lingüística Aplicada* 3: 146–157.

Puhr, T. (2017). Identity-Construction and Language-Deconstruction: Code-switching, Syntactic Experimentation, and Self-Translation in Vladimir Nabokov's *Lolita*, *Pnin*, and *King, Queen, Knave*. MA thesis, Northeastern Illinois University.

Rezaei, S., & Tadayyon, M. (2018). Linguistic landscape in the city of Isfahan in Iran: The representation of languages and identities in Julfa. *Multilingua*. 37(6): 701–720. 10.1515/multi-2017-0031.

Romaine, S. (1995). *Bilingualism*. New York: Basil Blackwell, Inc.

Sankoff, D., & Poplack, S. (1981). A formal grammar for codeswitching. *Papers in Linguistics*. 14, 3–46.

Scotton, C. M., & Ury, W. (1977). Bilingual strategies: The social functions of code-switching. *International Journal of Sociolinguistics*. 1977(13): 5–20.

Sebba, M., Mahootian, S., & Jonsson, C. (Eds.). (2012). *Language Mixing and Codeswitching: Approaches to Mixed Language Written Discourse*. Abingdon, UK: Routledge.

Stenson, N. (1990). Phrase structure congruence, government, and Irish-English code-switching. In: R. Hendrick (Ed.), *Syntax and Semantics 23* (pp. 167–197). New York: Academic Press, Inc.

Temple, C., & Christian, D. (2006). Applied social dialectology. In: U. Ammon, N. Dittmar, K.J. Mattheier, & P. Trudgill (Eds.), *Sociolinguistics: An International Handbook of the Science of Language and Society* (pp. 2546–2555). Berlin, Germany: Walter de Gruyter.

Timm, L. (1975). Spanish-English code-switching: el por quey how-not-to. *Romance Philology*. 28, 473–482.

Toribio, A. J. (2002). Spanish-English code-switching among US Latinos. *International Journal of the Sociology of Language*. 158, 89–119.

Toribio, A. J. (2011). Code-switching among US Latinos. In: Díaz-Campos, Manuel (Ed.), *The Handbook of Hispanic Sociolinguistics* (pp. 530–552). Oxford, UK: Blackwell Publishing Ltd.

Vogel, S., & Garcia, O. (2017). *Translanguaging*. Oxford Research Encyclopedia of Education. doi: 10.1093/acrefore/9780190264093.013.181.

Waring, C.D.L. (2018). Black and biracial Americans wouldn't need to code-switch if we lived in a post-racial society. https://theconversation.com/black-and-biracial-americans-wouldnt-need-to-code-switch-if-we-lived-in-a-post-racial-society-101013.

Zhang, Y., Wang, T., Huang, P., Li, D., Qiu, J., Shen, T., & Xie, P. (2015). Free language selection in the bilingual brain: An event-related fMRI study. *Scientific Reports*. 5: Article number: 11704.

Read and Watch

Contact and borrowing: Read about the origins of an expression we all use multiple times a day in Kumari Devarajan's article, "Ready For A Linguistic Controversy? Say 'Mmhmm'" www.npr.org/sections/codeswitch/2018/08/17/606002607/ready-for-a-linguistic-controversy-say-mhmm

African-American English and codeswitching--Excerpts from interviews made for the documentary TALKING BLACK IN AMERICA www.talkingblackinamerica.org

Part of The Language & Life Project. Published on Aug 18, 2017. www.youtube.com/watch?v=VpLQmyS7-jw

Non-threatening POC—The Cost of Code Switching | Chandra Arthur | TEDxOrlando www.youtube.com/watch?v=Bo3hRq2RnNI

Chapter 4

Childhood Bilingualism

Bilingual language acquisition is the simultaneous acquisition of more than one language during the developmental stages of language acquisition. Jules Ronjat's (1913) examination of his son Louis's simultaneous acquisition of French and German was the first detailed and documented study of a child exposed to and acquiring two languages simultaneously. Ronjat spoke only French to his son, while his wife spoke only German with him. This first foray into documenting bilingual language development was followed by a number of other longitudinal studies. Of particular significance is Leopold's meticulous documentation of his daughter Hildegard's acquisition of German and English. Published as a detailed four-volume diary (1939–1949), Leopold's study marked the beginning of focused interest in child bilingualism. Since then, others have conducted numerous studies, from detailed diaries spanning several years to experiments conducted in language labs. Five main questions dominate the field:

- How do children become bilingual?
- At what age do children start to differentiate between their two languages?
- Does being raised bilingually affect the natural path of language acquisition?
- Does being raised bilingually affect cognitive development?
- What does it mean when children codeswitch?

Thinking Matters

Take a few moments to consider each of these five questions and jot down some ideas to compare with the information presented in this chapter.

If you found it difficult to answer any of these questions, you are not alone. Though they may seem straightforward, to answer any one of them we must first look at what we know about babies and their general language capacity. After nearly a century of observational and experimental research in natural and in laboratory settings, here are some of the important facts we've come to know about babies and their language acquisition process. As early as within their first few months, infants are already showing signs of communicative readiness and intent:

- Upon birth, infants can pick their mother's voice out of other voices heard around them.
- Infants pay attention to faces. Frank, Vul, and Johnson (2008) found that infants as young as three months of age prefer faces and face-like stimuli over other visual stimuli. Many researchers maintain that this preference along with other early signs of communicative readiness plays an important role in infants' language development. We will learn more about this point later in the chapter.
- Research indicates that infants are aware of the interactive, social nature of language. For example, they are responsive to language when it is spoken to them and appear to 'take turns' in conversation as early as three months by cooing, flailing their arms, and kicking their legs in response to caretaker's vocalizations. And, by the age of one, infants have specific conversational expectations from their caretakers.

Thinking Matters

Watch this short video between a mother and an almost one-year-old as the mother "breaks" their conversational rules. Can you figure out what the child expected? https://www.youtube.com/watch?v=apzXGEbZht0.

- Infants as young as six weeks can discriminate between some voiced and voiceless sounds. For example, they can distinguish between the pairs of sounds [d] and [t], [b] and [p], and [g] and [k]. In addition, during most of the first year of life infants can distinguish sounds not present in the home language(s).
- By six months, infants begin to show the ability to categorize the sounds and intonation patterns of their own home language and are able to distinguish them from sounds of other languages. For example, experiments show that an infant growing up in a French household is more interested in listening to French than to English. By 12 months, infants stop using non-native sounds in their cooing and babbling, and restrict their babbling to the sounds of their home language.

This last point is particularly interesting in the context of bilingual language acquisition and carries with it implications for a brain prepared for multilingual input. In Section 4.1 we address how children become bilingual. In Section 4.2, we learn about experimental procedures used to ascertain infants' language capabilities. In Sections 4.3 and 4.4 we learn more about children's abilities to differentiate between their languages, and the cognitive effects of bilingual language acquisition. In our final Section, 4.5, we look at the significance of children's codeswitching.

Methodological considerations There are three important points to keep in mind as you read this chapter. First, nearly all of the research in the area of bilingual language acquisition and development has been conducted and continues to be conducted with children exposed to two languages. This is not a criticism; it's a fact. Therefore, in this chapter the term 'bilingual' really refers to a child raised with two languages and does not refer to a plurilingual. Many of the reasons that have confined the studies to two languages are practical, logistical reasons, such as the difficulty in finding participants who share the same three or more languages. There are also academic reasons: until we understand more about how two languages affect the infant and growing brain, it is best to not muddy the waters with additional languages, or other social factors.

A second methodological consideration is the notion of what it means, practically, to be raised bilingually. For the most part, there is no consensus across the studies as to what constitutes a bilingual household beyond the use of two languages. This means that a child receiving 70% of their language in language A and 30% in language B may be in the same study as the child receiving the reverse with the same two languages, or in a 50–50 split, and so on. Moreover, the number of speakers from each language the child sees regularly is not always taken into account, nor is the amount of time the child is exposed to media in each language. Further, the quality of the media itself is an important contributing factor to children's language development. For example, reading books to a child in one language and setting them in front of a TV in the other language constitutes two different types of language experience. Reading is active and interactive and often involves word repetition, asking questions, and providing expansions on topics. Screen time is mostly passive and rarely verbally interactive. In the case of the latter, the child has few opportunities to practice the language.

Along these lines, Suzanne Carroll (2017) cautions against hasty conclusions and suggests we need to ask more "subtle questions". She points out that "language" has been used somewhat interchangeably with *parts* of language: vocabulary acquisition is not the same as the acquisition of *language* with all of its subsystems (e.g., sound, words, syntax, and meaning). Importantly, she also points out that different types of exposure will affect different kinds of bilinguals differently.[1] Her points, aptly, are that (a) input/exposure alone is not the key to bilingual language development, that other external factors also need to be considered, and (b) we need to be aware of how the terminology used does not mean the same things across fields or even across researchers in the same fields.

A third point to keep in mind is that many of the experiments conducted with bilingual infants and children were originally developed with monolingual infants and children in mind.[2] This means that factors such as those mentioned in connection with the first two methodological issues may have been overlooked during the process of data collection.

4.1 How do Children Become Bilingual? Is There a Right Way to Raise Children Bilingually?

Thinking Matters

Before reading the next section, write down three of your own ideas to answer the two questions posed in the title of this section.

(Source: Khomich Yauheni, Shutterstock)

Fundamentally, children need a compelling reason to acquire more than one language. They must value the role each language plays in their lives, and grasp how each language helps them to achieve specific goals. The goals may be abstract and emotional, such as maintaining a relationship with monolingual family members, or they may be concrete and practical, like playing with the monolingual neighborhood kids. The most successful methods for achieving bilingualism rely on both languages serving important social, psychological, and emotional functions in the child's life, and the child having opportunities in various contexts to interact with each language. In other words, there is a bonding aspect that must be satisfied—each language should provide an opportunity for the child to connect and bond with a subset of the people and events in their life that can only be achieved through that specific language. The following two approaches have been able to capture both the practical and the emotional/psychological dimensions of growing up bilingual:

1. The one person, one language method, first proposed in 1902 by French linguist Maurice Grammont, remains a successful approach. Here, each parent attempts to consistently use only one of the household languages with the child at all times. Additionally, the parents only use their designated language when speaking to each other in the child's presence so that the child doesn't figure out that both parents, can speak both languages. The infant is thus exposed to both languages from birth and acquires

both simultaneously. Each language is a direct link between the child and one of their caretakers.

2. A second approach, the home language-public language method, is easier for most families to manage. The line between the two languages is drawn at the front door—the home language is used exclusively (to the extent possible) at home and the public language is used exclusively outside of the home. Here, the child often acquires their languages sequentially; home language first from birth, later followed by the public language through daycare, preschool, neighborhood kids, and so on. This second approach may also be combined with the one person, one language approach if the home languages are different from the public language. Let's keep in mind, though, that realistically, in this sequential method, the child is exposed to the public language, even if minimally, through television, out on shopping trips, and at restaurants and other public venues where the majority language is used. Ultimately, what's important is that the language that is the least represented across the various public domains get some exclusive time and attention, and that the caregivers in the child's life value bilingualism. Fantini (1985) provides a detailed record of her son Mario's bilingualism where the home language was Spanish and the public language was English.

These are just two broad examples of conditions conducive to bilingual development. There are many other combinations that can achieve the same results, as long as both languages are accessible and represented as equally important to the child. Accessibility includes providing fun and play in both languages. For instance, books should be read to the child and be available for the child to read in both languages. Other media such as videos, films, music, and so on should also be in both languages as much as possible. Moreover, games and other play activities, whether hide and seek or board games, can easily be provided in both languages. All-in-all, the point is to provide plenty and various types of language events for the child and to form emotional and social ties with the child through each language. Anecdotally, I know of bilingual adults who acquired their home language because it was the language their parents used when they wanted to keep conversations private, hence providing an incentive for the children to learn the 'secret' language!

It should be noted, however, that becoming a bilingual as a child does not guarantee that one remains bilingual in adulthood. To maintain bilingualism, the same motivations and conditions that encourage bilingualism in the first place need to be present throughout one's life. In other words, the speaker needs to perceive a need for each of the languages—whether for the sake of relationships, work, or leisure. Remember the two bilingually raised children Louis Ronjat and Hildegard Leopold mentioned earlier? Both children grew up bilingually in a one-parent, one-language fashion. Louis, who grew up with French and German in Paris, remained bilingual, using both languages easily (at least until the age of 15, after which we have no documentation of his language use). In contrast, Hildegard, who was raised in an English-German household, became English-dominant after age five, when she attended school in English in the United States (US). As mentioned in earlier chapters, bilingualism is not a static state of being. Rather, the relationship between the bilingual's languages is on a continuum and in flux, with dominance shifting from one to the other as circumstances, locales, and the people in the bilingual's life change.

An apt example comes from a study conducted by Mougeon and Beniak (1991), of French-English bilingual children growing up in the predominantly monolingual English-speaking community and households of Pembroke, Canada. Though the bilingual children were educated in French from the age of five, they still made numerous errors with their French reflexive pronouns (such as 'myself', 'herself', etc.), even as late as the 12th grade. These results show that the amount of input alone does not tip the scales toward one language or the other. Instead, as Carroll (2017) points out, the results reinforce the significance of the connection of French to the children's lives. Given that only 8% of the population in Pembroke was French-speaking at the time of the survey, and the children's home language was mostly English even when there was a French-speaking parent in the home, it's no surprise that the children identified with and valued English more than French. (See Chapter 3 for discussions of language choice and identity.)

Although Carroll's analysis has much merit, to be fair, we need to also recognize that in those first five years when the children in the study grew up with mostly English, it was not just their values and identities that became English-speaker-oriented. Rather, their grammatical 'settings' became solidly English by the time they started kindergarten. Unlike the case of sequential bilinguals in the US who come with minority home languages (such as Hindi, Spanish, Korean) into the majority public language (English), the Pembroke children were moving from a majority community language (English) into a minority community language (French). We can speculate that given the predominance of English in all other parts of their lives, including with friends and peers at school, there was no communicative or social urgency for the children to learn and use all aspects of French perfectly.

4.2 Understanding the Bilingual Brain: How Do We Know What Babies Know?

Some of the most difficult research to undertake is figuring out what goes on in babies' brains. Before we look at more research results, it's worthwhile to understand how linguists and psychologists study the language capabilities of infants, whether monolingual or bilingual, when they are still too young to produce speech. It's difficult to imagine the amount of information captured by such tiny and fragile beings before they even utter their first words. As we learned earlier, infants as young as six weeks old can tell the difference between very similar sounds such as b/p. Researchers in the fields of language development have found some creative and fruitful methods to measure both receptive and productive language. In the prelingual stage, before children speak their first words, there are four methods that are frequently used to ascertain their comprehension abilities. For example, to see whether and at what age children can distinguish different language sounds, tones, languages, or stress, researchers may use the **High Amplitude Sucking** procedure (HAS). Another procedure is the **Visual Fixation Procedure** (VFP), which is used to understand infants' word acquisition development. Both HAS and VFP rely on the concept of **habituation**, the "get used to it" concept. Habituation is a learning process where response to a stimulus decreases after the infant has been exposed to it repeatedly. Basically, the infant gets bored and stops paying attention to the object/sound/visual stimulus. Go to www.youtube.com/watch?v=dlilZh60qdA to watch a demonstration of habituation.

High Amplitude Sucking is used with infants from birth to four months. The infant wears a headphone and sucks on a pacifier hooked

(Source: Adrian Niederhaeuser, Shutterstock)

up to a pressure gauge. As the infant sucks energetically (high-amplitude sucking), they are "rewarded" with a sound over a loudspeaker, for example the sound 'ta'. Once the infant gets used to the sound and gets bored, the sucking declines and the infant is presented with a new sound, for example 'da'. If the infant has been able to distinguish the new sound from the previous one, his/her rate of sucking increases again, signaling interest in the new sound.

The **Visual Fixation Procedure**, like the HAS procedure, relies on habituation. In the VFP, the length of time the infant fixes his or her gaze on an object projected on a screen is measured, while the infant receives some language input, such as a sound, syllable, or word. Once infants get used to the sound-image pair, they turn away from the image. For example, infants show their awareness of a new sound, a new word, or a new language by an increase in the amount of time looking at what is presented on the screen. Elizabeth Johnson and Tania Zamuner (2010, p. 76) explain the procedure:

> In a typical study, participants sit on their caregiver's lap and watch a checkerboard (or some other simple visual stimulus) paired on each trial with a sound (e.g., a repeating syllable). In the beginning, both the sound and checkerboard are very interesting to the child. However, as time goes on, the sound and checkerboard become less interesting and infants gradually decrease their time looking at the screen. Infants are considered habituated by a preset criterion once they decrease their looking time at the checkerboard.

They are then presented with the checkerboard paired with a new token of the same sound (e.g., new token of same syllable) or a new sound (e.g., new token of new syllable). If infants can discriminate the two sounds, then they will be more interested in the new sound than the old sound, i.e., they will show their interest as indicated by an increase in their looking time at the checkerboard.

Two other procedures commonly used with infants are the **Head-Turn Procedure** and the **Preferential Looking Procedure** (PLP).

Go to the following links to watch demonstrations of the High Amplitude Sucking and Head-Turn procedures:

Ling Space: How to test language in babies shows babies during High-Amplitude Sucking and Head-Turn procedures at www.youtube.com/watch?v=3-A9TnuSVa8.

The Baby Human - Werker - Ba/Da Study at www.youtube.com/watch?v=Ew5-xbc1HMk.

Go to the links after this paragraph to watch sound discrimination experiments using the head-turn procedure. In each, infants who are being raised in monolingual English homes are exposed to languages they have never heard before. In the first video, using sounds from Hindi, psychologist Janet Werker (2014) shows infants raised in monolingual English-speaking homes distinguishing between Hindi and English sounds. In the second video, Werker (2006) does the same experiment using consonants from Nlaka'pamux, a First Nations Salishan language spoken in parts of British Columbia (also known as the Thompson language). Both Hindi and Nlaka'pamux have consonants that do not exist in English and cannot be distinguished by adult monolingual English speakers. The infants in the experiment had not been exposed to these consonants prior to the experiment. Through these experiments, Werker demonstrates that the infant's brain is capable of distinguishing sounds from any language without previous exposure to the language, an ability that the adult brain does not have. The relevance of these findings and that of similar studies for bilingual language acquisition is that they point to the infant brain as a multilingual brain, open to and capable of perceiving and distinguishing the sounds of a variety of languages from infancy.

Hindi: www.youtube.com/watch?v=WvM5bqUsbu8.
Nlaka'pamux: www.youtube.com/watch?v=WXWGnryjEaY.

One last important procedure is the **switch approach**. This procedure is often used to determine whether an infant has learned a new word. For a detailed explanation see Appendix I.

Now that we know how data is collected in infant language research, in the next sections we'll take a closer look at research results as we address the remaining two questions posed earlier: At what age do children start to differentiate between their two languages? And what does it mean when children codeswitch?

4.3 When Do Children Begin Differentiating between Their Two Languages?

At what point in their development simultaneous bilinguals differentiate between their two languages is a question that has been of interest to psychologists, linguists, psycholinguists, and parents alike. For the psycholinguist, the answer to this complicated question may shed light on general issues of linguistic and cognitive development as well as language processing and storage. For the linguist, it could provide evidence in favor of or against innate linguistic predispositions and the existence of language universals. And for parents, it could address any concerns about whether they run the risk of confusing their children or delaying their language acquisition by exposing them to multiple languages. The latter seems to be a concern that is more prevalent in the US, where bilingualism has been much less common than in other parts of the world where children are routinely exposed to more than one language successfully and without harm.

(Source: Sangoiri, Shutterstock)

Early on, two hypotheses were proposed to address bilingual language acquisition and the age at which children raised in bilingual households distinguish between their languages. The first, the **Unitary Language Hypothesis,** proposed that children initially perceive the input from the two languages as part of a single (unitary) language system, specifically as a single lexicon (Volterra and Taeschner, 1978). Over time, and through a three-stage process, the two languages would become separated and understood by the child to be two individual languages lexically and structurally. The first stage would end around age three. In stage two, the child would begin to separate out the vocabulary of the two languages, but the grammatical rules would remain in a single undifferentiated system. In the final stage, the child would separate out and differentiate between the grammatical rules of the two languages and thus be recognized as bilingual. Volterra and Taeschner do not offer a precise timeline for the completion of the second and third stages. And although their premise seems reasonable, there is little to no cognitive developmental or linguistic evidence to support a unitary hypothesis.

An alternate hypothesis, the **Dual System Hypothesis**, also called the **Independent Language System Hypothesis** of bilingual language acquisition, proposes that multiple languages are distinguished as separate systems from the beginning of the child's life (Genesee, 1989; Meisel 1989; De Houwer 1990). Overall, the research of the last two decades strongly favors a dual-system model. In fact, there's a large body of research which concludes that when exposed to two languages from birth, infants can distinguish their two languages and go on to develop two autonomous phonological, lexical, and grammatical systems.[3]

That said, one of the remaining complicated questions is whether children exposed to two languages from infancy acquire all the components of *both* languages (i.e., phonology, morphology, grammar) at the same rate as monolingual children. Spoiler alert: At this point it appears that they may not. When bilingual children's skills in only one of their languages are compared to that of monolinguals of the same language, the bilingual child's development appears to lag behind that of the monolingual's. However, and this is a very important 'however', overall these studies show that when their language development across the two languages is combined, children raised as simultaneous bilinguals achieve the same milestones at the same rate and time as monolinguals. Specifically, when measured across the two languages combined, the rate and number of words bilinguals acquire, the ability to combine words to make two-word phrases, and the acquisition of grammatical features such as plural and past tense, are equal to the rate of monolinguals' linguistic developments in the same areas.

Though children raised bilingually do not lag behind when both language achievements are taken together, they may lag behind in terms of vocabulary and grammatical development in their individual languages when compared to monolinguals of those same languages. These deficits are easily overcome (at least for the school language) once the child starts school, which means educators need to be aware that any seeming shortcoming is due to lack of exposure to the language, not because of developmental issues. In their study of Spanish-English bilingually developing children, Hoff, Core, Place, Rumiche, Señor, and Parra (2012) followed the language development of 47 children exposed to Spanish and English from birth and 56 monolingual children exposed only to English, at three age intervals: 1;10 (1 year and 10 months), 2;1 (2 years and 1 month), and 2;6 (2 years and 6 months). All families resided in South Florida and shared the same upper socioeconomic status (SES). From a comparison of various language milestones, Hoff et al. demonstrated that the difference between monolingual and bilingual children's grammatical skills in either of their languages depended on how much of each language the child heard. They note that:

Because the range of variation in both monolingual and bilingual development is large and because most bilingual children hear more of one language than the other, many bilingual children have single-language skills within the normal range of variation for monolinguals, particularly in their stronger language.

(p. 23)

Read on for the exciting details and insights into what we know about bilingually raised infants' and toddlers' language capacities.

4.3.1 Evidence for the Independent Language Hypothesis

In the following sections, we take a closer look at some of the studies that provide evidence of separate and mostly autonomous language systems in the early phases of bilingual language development.

Differentiating between languages by rhythm and sound—Some of the support for separate language systems comes from studies which focused on bilingual infants' ability to discriminate between languages based on the distinct stress patterns of each of their languages. In one study, psychologists Bosch and Sebatien-Galles (2001) compared the stress-discrimination abilities of 4.5-month-old infants who were raised in either monolingual Catalan- or Spanish-speaking households with the same age infants who were raised in Catalan-Spanish households. Bosch and Sebatien-Galles were able to show that by 4.5 months of age Spanish and Catalan monolingual infants and Spanish-Catalan bilingual infants were equally able to discriminate between the two languages. They concluded that the bilingual infants' regular exposure to the two languages did not hamper their ability to distinguish each language as a separate system. The bilingual infants responded the same way as the monolingual infants, reacting to each language as a new stimulus. Bosch and Sebatien-Galles further concluded, "These results can be taken as initial evidence of an early capacity to distinguish languages in simultaneous bilingual exposure, thus challenging the hypothesis that language discrimination capacities are delayed in bilinguals" (2001, p. 29).

In 2016, Naja Ferjan Ramírez at the Institute for Learning and Brain Sciences at the University of Washington reported an exciting new finding in support of a multilingual-ready brain. Ferjan Ramírez discovered that 11-month-old infants raised in bilingual Spanish-English households showed different brain activity when exposed to Spanish than infants raised in monolingual English-speaking households. Half of the babies participating were raised in bilingual Spanish-English households while the other half were growing up in monolingual English-speaking households. Using magnetoencephalography (MEG), Ferjan Ramírez and her team measured brain responses in the infants and found that the bilingually raised babies showed responses to both Spanish and English sounds, while the monolingual infants' brains only responded to English sounds. These results strongly favor a brain which is multilanguage-capable at birth.

Thinking Matters

Watch this brief video in which Dr. Ferjan Ramírez describes her research and demonstrates her experiment. What is an additional finding that Dr. Ramírez and her team obtained? www.youtube.com/watch?v=N7Gn_lmK4_Y.

Grammatical development and language differentiation—Other studies have examined the relationship between the size of the bilingual child's vocabulary in each language and grammatical development in each of their languages. The goal of these studies was to discover (1) whether for bilingual children as for monolingual children, a larger vocabulary predicted greater grammatical development, and (2) whether vocabulary size in just one of the child's languages would predict grammatical development in both of the child's languages.

These studies found that for bilinguals as with monolinguals, a larger vocabulary did in fact predict a more developed grammar.[4] Additionally, and directly relevant to the question of one grammar or two, the studies found that the benefits of a large vocabulary in one of the languages did not cross over to the other language. In other words, a larger vocabulary in Spanish predicted a more developed Spanish grammatical system for the bilingual Spanish-English speaking child, but it could not predict the child's grammatical development in English. Proficiency and skills in one did not predict the same levels in the other language. In the same vein, if one of the bilingual child's languages was less developed, it did not interfere with the development and progress of the child's other language.

Subsequently, these studies concluded that the bilingual child's two languages were separate systems. Moreover, they proposed that the quality of the language the child is exposed to may be more important than the quantity of language they hear—that is to say, the language which provides the child with a rich variety of language experiences is the language in which the child develops more vocabulary and consequently more developed grammatical skills.

Translation Equivalents and Language Differentiation—One of the arguments Unitary Language Hypothesis proponents use to support their hypothesis is young bilingual children's (frequent) lack of **translation equivalents** between their two languages. For instance, they may produce the word 'give' in one language, but not produce the equivalent word in the other. Consequently, they claim that a lack of equivalents indicates a single language system in which **mutual exclusivity** prohibits them from accepting more than one label per item. **The mutual exclusivity constraint** (MEC) is the long-held theory that infants expect each item in their world to have only one name. Evidence in favor of the MEC comes from experiments where a child is shown two items, one the child knows the name of and an unfamiliar, usually made-up item. When the child is asked to point to the "nop", they pick the hitherto unknown object. In other words, they never expect that the known item could have more than one name. Based on that assumption, they choose the new item to be the "nop". Watch this short video which demonstrates the notion of mutual exclusivity with two monolingual toddlers, a 1.5-year-old boy and a two-year-old girl: www.youtube.com/watch?v=FAEE2UULdq0.

Based on the MEC, the expectation would naturally be that bilingually raised infants of the same age would also expect each item to have only one name and would consequently reject a second word for the same item. However, that is not the case. Houston-Price, Caloghiris, and Raviglione (2010) conducted an important and elucidating experiment which showed that unlike their monolingual counterparts, bilingually raised infants between the ages of 17 and 22 months did not show a preference for the unknown object in MEC tasks when presented with an unknown word (e.g., "where's the 'nop'?" or "show me the 'nop'").

They conclude that, as a result of hearing multiple names for the same object, bilingually raised babies do not adhere to the mutual exclusivity strategy: they don't assume that a new word means a new object. Consequently, they are able to accept more than one name for any item. This cognitive flexibility helps to explain why a bilingual English-Spanish speaking child could have both *libro* (Spanish) and *book* (English) for 'book' without confusion. So it appears that bilingual children are able to accept more than one word for an item. Therefore, Houston-Price and colleagues conclude that the notion of mutual exclusivity is a conditioned, learned behavior and not an innate feature of the linguistic brain. They also conclude that since bilingual infants are not raised to expect a one-to-one relationship between words and objects, they are able to build two separate lexicons, one for each of their languages.

Results from other research corroborate Houston et al.'s findings and conclusions. In the following section, we will see that case studies also provide language-use evidence in favor of the Independent Systems Hypothesis and counter to the Mutual Exclusivity Constraint.

Socio-pragmatic support for differentiated language systems— Other researchers have approached the language differentiation question from a socio-pragmatic angle, asking whether bilingually raised children have social awareness of their two languages. Can they use the correct language in the correct context, with the correct speakers? Results of early case studies such as those by Ronjat and by Leopold, and of more recent ones such as those conducted by Fantini, Baum,

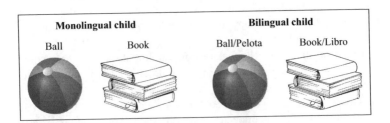

Figure 4.1 For children raised bilingually, mutual exclusivity is not an issue. The bilingual child can accept two words for the same object.

(Source: Boyko.Pictures, Shutterstock; & Neizu, Shutterstock)

Genesee, and Lanza, showed that even very young children were able to use language "appropriately" by matching the language of the person they were interacting with and even using the language-appropriate onomatopoetic words.[5]

Suzanne Baum's study (1997) was particularly important because of the children's ages. In a year-long longitudinal study, Baum observed two young children, Carlos at 1;3 and Andrew at 1;6 at the start of the study, who were being brought up in separate Spanish-English bilingual households. At the outset of her study, Baum established that each child understood both languages when spoken to in each language. This was an important first step to establish that the children understood two sets of grammar rules and had two sets words for many of the same objects (as long as they had heard the word in both languages). She further found that the children distinguished between their two languages, which they demonstrated by responding and using English with the monolingual English-speaking caretaker and the researcher while using Spanish with the Spanish-speaking parent, and codeswitching when the parent did so. Here are excerpts of conversations with Carlos at 1;3 and Andrew at 1;6 (from Baum 1997, pp. 94–97). I've underlined the Spanish words to eliminate confusion.

Carlos (C) interacting with Mother (M) and Observer (O):
C: Ahhhh! (Playing, falls)
M: <u>Upa!</u> (lifting him up) <u>¿Qué pasó?</u> (What happened?)
      <u>Pasame la pelota</u> (Pass me the ball) (Mother has hands out)
C: (Carlos hands Mother the ball. Mother gives him back the ball.)

Later, with the Observer
O: Throw me the ball.
C: (Carlos throws the ball to the observer) Heeee

This exchange tells us that Carlos has translation equivalents for 'the ball', 'me', and possibly for 'give'. It also shows that Carlos, at age 1;3, has receptive syntactic knowledge of both languages, enough to understand simple commands in both languages.

In the next exchange, Andrew at 1;6 is recorded at his monolingual English-speaking caretaker's home. Caretaker (C), Andrew (A).

C: Show me your book.
A: (Gives her the book).
C: Give me the car. Where should I put the car?
A: (Guides her hand to the garage).
C: Give Suzanne a kiss.
A: (Gives the researcher a kiss.)

In the next exchange, Andrew shows comprehension of equivalent Spanish and English vocabulary and grammar. Father (F), Andrew (A):

F: <u>Dale un beso a mama.</u> [Give mom a kiss)
A: (Andrew gestures toward mother and blows her a kiss.)
F: ¿Quieres leer un libro? [Do you want to read a book?] <u>Oye, ¿por qué, no traes un libro?</u> [Listen, why don't you get a book?] <u>Traeme un libro.</u> [Bring me a book].
A: (Andrew goes to his room and brings back a book.)

In Andrew's interactions, just as with Carlos's, we see evidence in favor of independent, separated language systems: a young child manages two languages lexically and syntactically. Moreover, in both Carlos's and Andrew's responses we have clear evidence that mutual exclusivity (one word per object) does not hold. On the contrary, children in the earliest phases of lexical development are able to acknowledge and accept more than one label for a given item.

Furthermore, in the next conversation we see Andrew using his two languages resourcefully as he tries to get his message across to his English-only caretaker. In this exchange, Andrew is playing with cars and trying to put them all in a toy garage. Andrew (A), Caretaker (C).

A: Rara. (Playing with cars. He tries to put them all in the garage)
C: What are you doing? (She hands him toy keys. He gives her a car.)
A: Alga. (He just put all the cars in the garage of the playhouse.)
C: That's not "all gone". (At this point, the caretaker is watching TV and is not paying attention.)
A: Hmmm. Hmmm. (Trying to close garage door)
C: What?
A: Der [there].
C: (No response from caretaker.)

A: <u>Ayi</u>. [ahí=there]
C: What? Oh, you want to close the door ...

Baum attributes Andrew's switch into Spanish to frustration and attention-getting on his part, a strategy that worked when the caretaker failed to respond to his utterance in English. It's also noteworthy that the children in Baum's study, though receiving different amounts of each language, in different contexts, and from different people, were nevertheless able to acquire the vocabulary and syntax of the two languages and keep them separate.

Differences between monolingual and bilingual infants' languages processing strategies—Still other studies concluded that infants exposed to more than one language develop different language processing strategies than do infants raised in monolingual households, leading the researchers to reason that infants raised bilingually maintain a distinction between their language systems from early on. Look at the four photographs in Figure 4.2 of mothers interacting with their babies. Write down everything you notice about the photos. Do you see any commonality across the four mother-baby pairs?

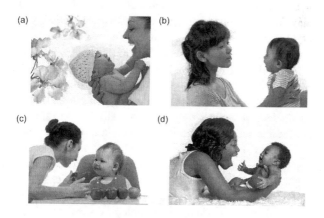

Figure 4.2 Mothers interacting with their babies.

(Source: Leonid and Anna Dedukh, Shutterstock; leolintang, Shutterstock; Oksana Kuzmina, Shutterstock; & Kim Ruoff, Shutterstock)

You may have noticed that:

a. Each mother's face is very close to her baby's face.
b. Each baby is looking intently at his or her mother's mouth.

There is ample evidence that infants, whether raised as monolinguals or bilinguals, pay closer attention to faces and objects than to other things in their surroundings. When being talked to, infants are not only attending to the sounds they hear but are also paying attention to other information in their environments to help them understand what they are hearing. In the case of speech, it is the person's mouth that is of primary interest to the infant. This selective attention to faces has been linked to language development. Specifically, a number of studies have shown that attention to the mouth during infancy is linked to a larger vocabulary in toddlerhood.[6] Researchers interested in bilingualism have extended these discoveries in order to gain better understanding of bilingual language development. One such seminal study was conducted by Whitney Weikum and her colleagues (2007). Weikum and her colleagues were interested in seeing whether attention to speakers' mouths extended infants' abilities to distinguish between languages solely based on the visual properties of languages (the articulatory movements of the mouth, lips, and tongue needed to make various language sounds that lip-readers pay attention to for lip-reading[7]). Moreover, they were also interested in finding whether monolingual infants and bilingual infants were able to lip-read equally well. Through an ingenious experiment, Weikum and her colleagues discovered that bilingual infants and monolingual infants did not perform equally on the lip-reading language differentiation tasks. In fact, in contrast to monolingually raised infants, bilingual infants continued to distinguish between languages beyond eight months.

They started with monolingual Spanish and monolingual Catalan infants four to six months old, all of whom had been exposed to English. They found that when watching silent clips of bilingual French-English speakers, these infants were able to distinguish when the speakers used English and when they used French.

Next, they performed the same task with the monolingual infants at eight months of age and compared the results to those of eight-month-old bilingual infants from bilingual Spanish-Catalan-speaking homes. Weikum et al. discovered three things:

(a) the bilingual infants who had never been exposed to either French or English paid more attention to the mouth of the speakers on the video than did the monolingual infants;
(b) the bilingual infants could differentiate between French and English;
(c) the monolingual infants, however, could no longer differentiate between English and French on the silent videos.

Weikum et al. concluded that bilingually raised babies use the visual aspects of speech articulation to process and keep their languages distinct from each other, hence the earlier and longer attention to the mouth by bilingual infants. Results such as these give strong support to the Independent System Hypothesis and provide insights into the cognitive similarities and differences between the monolingual and the bilingual brain.

Building on the Weikum et al. study, Pons, Bosch, and Lewkowitz (2015) found that even four-month-old infants raised bilingually pay more attention to mouths than do monolingually raised infants. Monolingual Spanish and monolingual Catalan infants and bilingual Spanish-Catalan infants were observed viewing videos in their native language (either Spanish or Catalan) and in English (a language that neither the monolingual or bilingual infants had heard before). They noted that the bilingually raised infants paid more attention to speakers' mouths than did the monolingually raised infants. Like Weikum and colleagues, they also hypothesized that the extra attention to the mouth was a developmental strategy to enhance language acquisition in multilingual contexts and that the additional attention to mouths provided visual cues infants used to determine which language they were hearing.

Byers-Heinlein, Morin-Lessard, and Lew-Williams (2017) also found compelling evidence of early language discrimination and language awareness among bilingually raised infants. By comparing adults' responses to those of infants, they concluded that bilingual infants, like bilingual adults, monitor which language they are hearing as they are listening, which in turn, Byers-Heinlein et al. hypothesize, allows bilinguals to activate the appropriate language while suppressing the other language. They further conclude that the activity of monitoring and controlling of their two languages explains why other research shows bilinguals possess a cognitive advantage in some tasks.

Overall, current studies of bilingual infants' language perception indicate that (a) simultaneous bilingual infants distinguish different language sounds as well as monolingually raised infants, (b) bilingually raised infants develop different strategies (such as extended attention to speakers' mouths) to help keep their languages separate, and (c) exposure to two languages can affect aspects of infants' cognitive systems and perhaps promote general cognitive advantages.

4.4 Does Being Raised Bilingually Affect the Natural Path of Language Acquisition?

According to Erika Hoff: "There is substantial evidence from the study of monolingually developing children that the amount of speech children hear is related to their rate of language development, supporting the view that language development is paced by children's access to input" (Hoff et al., 2012, p. 4).

Thinking Matters

Before reading the next section, take a moment to jot down what significance you think the quote from the Hoff et al. study holds for bilingual language acquisition. Do you think bilingual children acquire their languages at the same rate and within the same time frames as monolingually raised children? Explain your reasoning.

How does Hoff et al's statement apply to bilingualism in general? Recall our discussion of types of bilinguals and the notion of the "balanced bilingual" in Chapter 1 and the likelihood of such speakers roaming the earth. Our conclusion was that the balanced bilingual speaker is a rarity, if not an outright myth or ideal. In the context of language acquisition, the likelihood becomes even less. To become a balanced bilingual, the infant/young child would have had to receive the same amount and type of language input from both languages, including vocabulary, sentence types (active, passive, declarative, interrogative, and so on), use of tenses and so on, in the same contexts—a highly unlikely possibility.

The short answer to whether bilingual language acquisition affects language development is 'no'. Studies have concluded that the general stages of language development, from cooing to babbling, to the one-word, two-word, multi-word and clause stages, are accomplished within the same periods for both monolingually and bilingually raised children. Moreover, studies have also found that bilingual and monolingual children progress with the morphology and syntax of their languages, such as the acquisition of plurals and verb tense, within the same developmental time frames and stages. However, as we have already read, studies also show that the bilingual's two languages do not always develop in the same way or at the same time, and that some aspects may develop more quickly in one language than in the other. For example, the fact that children know how to make a plural noun in one of their languages doesn't mean they know how to also make plurals in their other language at the same point in their development. The difference in rate of development between the two languages will be greatly dependent on the *amount of exposure* the child has to each language and the quality of the language the child receives. For example, a child may hear less Spanish than English, but the Spanish he or she hears may be more complex, including novel words and more advanced grammatical structures, which will likely promote the child's acquisition of a larger vocabulary and more advanced grammar. Consequently, research has concluded that the child's two languages do not influence each other during development, nor do they hinder each other's natural development.

In a recent study to measure the effects of bilingualism on vocabulary development, two psychologists, Fennell and Byers-Heinlein (2014), conducted a study with two groups of 1.5-year-olds. Half of the babies were growing up in bilingual French-English households, while the other half were from monolingual English-speaking households. Using a switch approach method (described in the Appendix),

Fennell and Byers-Heinlein sought to determine whether monolingually and bilingually raised toddlers perform equally when learning new words where only the initial consonants are different (e.g., 'fit' and 'bit'). Fennell and Byers-Heinlein found that both monolingual and bilingual infants were equally sensitive to a change in the initial sounds of the presented words and were able to learn the new words successfully. For more details on the other interesting results of this study, you can go to www.psychologytoday.com/us/blog/life-bilingual/201708/bilingual-infants-learning-new-words.

4.5 Bilingualism and Cognitive Development: Cognitive Advantage or Cognitive Cost?

Cognitive development is the growth of the brain's ability to process information it receives through the senses and to use that information to think and to solve problems, from remembering to decision making. As children's brains develop, so do the **executive functions** of the brain—the set of cognitive processes needed to reason, to pay attention and keep focused on tasks, to learn new things, including language, and to form and retrieve memories. From birth onward, your brain works actively to create a storehouse of knowledge you use every day. Therefore, it is no surprise that one of the big questions psycholinguists ask is whether exposure to more than one language affects the natural course of the brain's development and executive functions.

As may be expected, research findings in this area are mixed. On the one hand, there is growing evidence in favor of positive effects on bilingually raised children's executive control and function.[8] However, there are also studies that show no executive function differences between multilingual and monolingual children.[9] Significantly, there are no studies that show that bilingual children's executive functions lag behind or suffer when compared with those of monolinguals. Though there is no final answer regarding the effects of bilingualism on the child's or adult's brain, there is no doubt that bilingualism has social and personal benefits, and there is increasing evidence that bilingualism may, in fact, enhance some processing activities.

Thinking Matters

Read the following exchanges. Each points to and is an example of **metalinguistic awareness**. Given these examples, see if you can write a definition for metalinguistic awareness.

Bilingual Mario, age 2;8, makes a remark about the language used when he gets on an airplane (from Fantini, 1985, p. 44):

Mario: Gente 'hello'en la'yon [meaning to say la gente dice 'hello' en la avion] = 'People say 'hello' on the airplane'

Later at the age of 3;4 Fantini reports that Mario picks out and comments on the Spanish name of a horse 'Amigo' (friend), while watching a horse race in English on television.

Exchange between nine-year-old Mario and monolingual nine-year-old Rodney, upon hearing Spanish-Mario and Carla speaking Spanish to each other (from Fantini, 1985, pp. 44 and 53):

Rodney: Hey what's wrong with you guys? Watcha speaking?
Mario: Spanish
Rodney to his mom: How come I can't speak like that?
Mario to Rodney: I can teach you for an hour. Will that be all right?
Rodney: Yeh

The conversations above between Mario and his mother, and Rodney and Mario serve as examples of what's referred to as metalinguistic awareness—the ability to talk about language and to monitor and analyze it apart from the meaning of its words and sentences. Mario has it as early as age 2;8 years. Mario is aware that more than one language exists and that different people use different languages. He also has expectations of which language should be used by whom and where.

Until recently, questions regarding the effects of bilingualism on cognitive development (including metalinguistic awareness) have been at the center of much controversy. Both Leopold (1949) and Ronjat (1913) maintained that bilingualism did not disadvantage their children and in fact imbued them with a metalinguistic awareness not shared by monolinguals of the same age. At the time, Leopold and Ronjat were a distinct minority in their support and understanding of childhood bilingualism. Much of early 20th century research that aimed at finding answers to this important question was deeply flawed and motivated by anti-immigration sentiments. These early studies, mostly conducted in the US in the 1920s and 1930s, concluded that bilingualism would have negative developmental and cognitive effects. These conclusions were based on the results of intelligence tests which were (and many still are) culture-specific. In the case of these early studies, the tests used were designed for a Northern European, educated, English-speaking population (e.g., the Stanford–Binet intelligence test). Consequently, all others who did not fit this bundle of characteristics performed poorly. In fact, sadly, those who should have known better were so influenced by the political anti-immigrant climate of the time that they abandoned good science and reason. For example, voices of abundant influence, important researchers, and educators such as educational psychologist Florence Goodenough, asserted that "the use of a foreign language in the home is one of the chief factors in producing mental retardation" (1926, p. 393). Other similarly baseless and unsupported determinations were made, such as associating bilingual language development with stuttering or predicting that a child exposed to more than one language would become semilingual, unable to form full thoughts or sentences in either language! It is astonishing that so much misinformation could thrive, despite the fact that a substantial percentage of the world's population was robustly bilingual.

Though these misguided assertions and folklore concerning the effects of bilingualism continued longer than they should have, in 1962, two Canadian researchers, Elizabeth Peal and Wallace E. Lambert, were able to bring rationality and rigor to bilingual language research. They conducted a study comparing the performance of ten-year-old bilingual French- and English-speaking children with that of ten-year-old monolingual English speakers on a series of standard tests of intelligence. Their results showed that the bilingual participants' performance was superior to that of the monolinguals in measures of verbal intelligence and in nonverbal tests which involved "concept-formation or symbolic flexibility" (p. 14). Peal and Lambert's study marked the beginning of a much more rigorous and careful examination of the cognitive effects of bilingualism.

Based on the last half-century of studies, not only have the previous negative and harmful reports on bilingualism been discredited but many researchers now believe that bilingualism brings with it a *cognitive advantage*. For example, a number of studies suggest that bilingualism may, in fact, enhance certain types of executive function in children and adults and promote and possibly increase a more analytical approach to language. About a dozen years after Peal and Lambert, John Cummins (1978) conducted a study with monolingual English and bilingual Irish-English third- and sixth-graders in Ireland (who matched in IQ, SES, gender, and age). He found that the bilingual children in both grades showed greater knowledge of certain aspects of language and performed better when evaluating contradictory statements.[10]

Two decades later in Stockholm, Jakob Cromdal conducted a similar study with Swedish-English bilingual and monolingual Swedish children who were six to seven years old. Results of his study, too, revealed an analytical advantage when children were asked to identify errors in four types of sentences. Cromdal (1999) concluded that the bilingual child's early need to compare and contrast the language input from their two languages starts the linguistic analysis process earlier in bilingual children, hence the results obtained from his study.[11]

Other research has focused on bilingual vocabulary acquisition. Here, too, as with the acquisition and maintenance of two sound systems, the main question is whether the bilingually raised infant will perform as well as the monolingually raised infant during the various stages of vocabulary acquisition. To provide some context, we should note that universally, regardless of language, infants *produce* their first words between 8 and 12 months of age. By 12 months, infants can use a few words meaningfully in context, though not always with adult-like pronunciation (parents, however, mostly understand what their child is referring to when they say 'ba' instead of 'ball', for example). Note that, at the same age, infants can already *understand* many words spoken to them. By 18 months, the average child can produce 10 to 20 words. Research shows that bilingually raised infants perform as well as monolingually raised infants with regards to total number of words used and understood at the same milestones.

Though the precise effects of bilingualism on children's cognitive development are mostly still unknown, we do know that bilingualism means linguistic, cognitive, and social adaptation and flexibility, and an increased capacity for abstract thinking. Moreover, these studies not only offer insights into bilingual language acquisition and cognition but also add to our knowledge of the brain's language capacity as a whole.

4.6 What Does It Mean When Children Codeswitch?

Thinking Matters

What are some reasons for children to codeswitch? Do they differ from adults' reasons for codeswitching? Will children's codeswitched utterances be similar to those of bilingual adults?

A further issue often debated, related to the question of whether bilingually raised infants start with unitary or independent language systems, is why young children codeswitch and what it may imply. Is it evidence of the unitary language system, i.e., children simply do not know they are using two languages because both are part of a single language bin? Is it because the child does not have the same vocabulary in both languages due to lack of equal input from both languages? Is it due to a phonological reason, such as one word being easier to say in one language than in the other? Or something else? The short answer is that, just as with adult codeswitching, there are linguistic, sociolinguistic, and psycholinguistic forces at work when children codeswitch. In the remainder of this chapter, we look at a mix of these variables and end the chapter by comparing children's and adults' codeswitches.

4.6.1 Is Codeswitching Evidence of a Unitary System?

As we discussed earlier, the main theoretical question for researchers is whether children start out with a unitary language system that gradually splits into two separate systems or whether they develop their two languages as two separate systems. Both groups have a vested interest in how codeswitching by young children is to be interpreted. Proponents of the Unitary System claim that codeswitching by young children indicates that the child's two languages are undifferentiated and therefore part of a single system. On the other hand, the Independent Language supporters assert that codeswitching is clear evidence of a child's ability to have mastery over his or her two (or more) languages, citing the child's appropriate socio-pragmatic language choices as indicative of each of the child's languages constituting a separate system. They claim that to show an undifferentiated system, a child would need to use the two languages randomly in the context of either language (e.g., a bilingual French-Chinese speaking child would have to use French with Chinese speakers and Chinese with French speakers).

Thinking Matters

What is your opinion? Is codeswitching evidence for a Unitary System or an Independent Language system? Explain your answer.

Thrown into this mix is the continued erroneous assumption by some, despite evidence to the contrary, that codeswitching in young children is due to poor cognitive control over their two languages. In other words, they are not able to keep them apart.[12] This assumption has not only been put to rest but, as we learned in Section 4.3, there is also evidence that codeswitching may, in fact, point to enhanced executive function control (paying attention, staying focused on tasks to completion, organizing, planning and prioritizing, able to understand different points of view, etc.). Moreover, codeswitching entails greater linguistic knowledge and heightened sensitivity to contextual cues. Baum (1997), Genesee (1989, 1995), and Lanza (1997), among others, found that bilingual children, even at the one-word stage, keep their languages separate by using them in the appropriate monolingual contexts, such as using the language others around them are speaking.

It is often assumed that bilingual children codeswitch because they know the word in one language but not the other. However, that's not always the case. "Knowing" can be receptive-only, productive, or both receptive and productive. You can know a language passively/receptively, in which case you understand and know the meaning of a word when you hear it. Or you can be a productive know-er, in which case you may use a word even when you don't really know the meaning or association—as for example like the one-year-old who refers to every male as 'dada' or uses 'blue' for all colors. For monolingual and bilingual children alike, their receptive vocabulary is larger than their productive vocabulary, especially during the early stages of language acquisition. Therefore, we should not rush to judgment and assume that since the bilingual Japanese-English child uses *cat* instead of *neko*, that they only know the word *cat* to refer to the animal. Complete mastery entails knowing a word when you hear it and producing appropriately when needed. Outside of a handful of studies, researchers have paid little attention to comprehension on its own. Typically, children's bilingualism, especially with young children and toddlers, is measured through production, i.e., what they can say meaningfully in each language. To codeswitch, speakers need to have a large degree of control over their languages. A recent study by Yow, Tan, and Flynne (2018) concludes that codeswitching by young children should not be interpreted as a lack of competence in their two languages. In their study, 56 bilingual Mandarin-English bilingual children aged five to six years were observed three hours per day over a five-day period while they performed normal classroom activities. Their results strongly suggest that codeswitching is a marker of linguistic competence.

In the next section we compare codeswitches made by children ages 2;2 years to 3;8 years to show that bilingual children use and combine their two languages in the same way as bilingual adults.[13] Codeswitching by adults is rule-governed and systematic, and the same is true of children's codeswitching.

4.6.2 Comparing Children's and Adults' Codeswitches

Examples (1)–(9) show mixed utterances in a variety of language pairs produced by children between the ages of 1;10, the beginning of the two-word stage in language development, and 3;4, when the child is making longer simple sentences and questions. The German-French / French-German examples are from Köppe & Meisel (1995, p. 22), the Norwegian-English are from Lanza (1997, p. 141), and the Russian-English examples are from O'Neill (1998). In all the examples, a switch into the other language is shown by underlining the word or phrase switched into. Note that the utterances in examples (1)–(7) were produced by children who are within the two-word stage of language development, a stage where nouns dominate the child's vocabulary.

(1) nein <u>canard</u>   (Ger-Fr, 1;10)
    no duck
(2) das <u>bateau</u>   (Ger-Fr, 2;0)
    This ship
(3) das <u>petit tigre</u>   (Ger-Fr, 2;0)
    'That little tiger'
(4) ça <u>sonne</u>   (Fr-Ger, 1;11)
    'This this sun'
(5) das <u>dort</u> ne?   (Ger-Fr, 2;0)
    'This sleeps, right?'
(6) deddy [<u>re</u>]sucht   (Ger-Fr, 2;4)
    'Teddy seeks again'
(7) mer <u>cookie</u>   (Norw-Eng, 2;2)
    'more cookie'

Examples (8) and (9) show more sophisticated switches, where free morphemes of one language (verbs) are accurately combined with suffixes of the other language.

(8) wash-<u>er ansiktet</u>   (Eng-Norw, 2;4)
    'washes the/her face'
(9) It's <u>lop</u> -en.   (Russ-Eng, 3;2)
    __break-_
    'It's broken.'

In addition to shedding light on the relationship between early child grammars and adult grammars, comparisons of child and adult codeswitches provide an additional testing ground for the various codeswitching models we discussed earlier. Based on the data we have, only principle-based models of codeswitching such as the Head-Complement Principle model (Mahootian, 1993, 96) and Myers-Scotten's Matrix Language Frame model, both described in Chapter 3, have been successfully applied to children's codeswitching data. In the following examples, (adapted from Mahootian, 2006), a comparison of adult codeswitches and children's codeswitches shows switches occurring at the same grammatical points (i.e., between determiners and noun phrases, verbs and objects, and so on) in both adults' and children's utterances. Languages and the children's ages are given in parentheses.

Switches between Determiner and NP

Switches between determiners (including articles, possessive pronouns, and deictics such as *this*, *that*, and *those*), and noun phrases are the most common across all language pairs. In example (10a), an adult Spanish-English bilingual switches from a Spanish determiner article *el* ('the') to the English noun phrase *same night*. Examples (10b) and (10c) show the same type of switch—between a determiner and a noun phrase—produced by young German-French and Russian-English bilingual children.

Adult
(10a) el <u>same night</u>   (Sp-Eng; Pfaff)
  the
  'the same night'

Child
10(b) das <u>petit tigre</u>   (Ger-Fr, 2;0)
  'That little tiger'
(10c) That's my <u>kino</u>.   (Russ-Eng, 3;4)
  cinema (movie)
  'That's my movie.'

Switches between Verb and Direct Object

In example (11a), the switch from French to Arabic takes place between the French verb *changer* ('change') and the Arabic object noun phrase *ttwSe:l* ('the receipt'). We see the same type of switch, in example (11b) between a Swedish verb *klappe* and the English object noun phrase *hand*, produced by a 2;2-year-old Swedish-English bilingual child.

Adult

(11a) il ne faut pas changer <u>ttwSe:l</u> (Fr-Arab, Bentahila and Davies, 1983)
                              the receipt
      'You must not change the receipt.'

Child

(11b) klappe <u>hand</u>   (2;2, Swed-Eng)
      clap
      'clap hand'

Switches between Subject and Verb Phrase

Examples (12a) and (12b) show switches between a subject pronoun
and the verb phrase. In (12a), the adult Russian-English speaker
switches from English 'you' to Russian for the verb phrase (govorish,
chto eto vozmozhno). In (12b), a 2;7-year-old Norwegian-English
bilingual child switches from the Norwegian subject pronoun *jeg* ('I')
into the English verb phrase *give it to daddy*.

Adult

(12a) No <u>you</u> govorish, chto eto vozmozhno.
         But you say that that possible
         'But you say that it's possible.' (Russ-Eng)

Child

(12b) Jeg <u>give it to daddy</u>
      I
      'I give it to daddy' (Norw-Eng, 2;7)

Switches between Verb and Prepositional Phrase

Examples (13a) and (13b) show switches in adult and child speech
between a verb in one language and a prepositional phrase in the other.
The sentence in (13a) was produced by an adult Russian-English bilingual and shows a switch between the Russian verb *zhil* ('lived') and the
English prepositional phrase *in a trailer*. In example (13b), a 3;7-year-
old German-French bilingual child produces the same type of switch

between a French verb and a German prepositional phrase *zum krank-enwagen* ('to the ambulance').

Adult

(13a) Nu vidish, <u>Steven King</u> zhil <u>in a trailer</u>.

     So you see   lived

     So you see, Steven King lived in a trailer.' (Russ-Eng, O'Neill, 1998)

Child

(13b) on va maintenant <u>zum</u> <u>krankenwagen</u>

     we go now   to the ambulance

     'We now go to the ambulance.' (Fr-Ger, 3;7, Meisel, 1994)

Switches between Roots and Affixes

In examples (14a) and (14b), we see switches between Russian and English, where the free root of one language is combined with a suffix from the other language.

Adult

(14a) Eto na-<u>dresser</u>-e.   (Russ-Eng)

     That on   Sg

     'It's on the dresser.'

Child

(14b) It's <u>lop</u> -en.   (Russ-Eng, 3;10)

     break-

     'It's broken.'

Comparisons of the pairs of examples in (10)–(14) reveal clear similarities between children's and adults' codeswitches. It appears that adult and child bilinguals have the same understanding of the grammatical relationship between their two languages, even in the earliest stages of grammatical development (such as the two-word stage). We know bilingual adults' two languages function as separate systems, and that adults are fully aware that they speak two or more languages.

We have also seen that adult codeswitches are grammatical and follow well-defined rules. They know which sounds and words belong to each of their languages. Members of bilingual speech communities can spontaneously and naturally communicate with each other in mixed-code speech, and in each of their languages separately. In short, we have no reason to question whether the bilingual adult's two languages are a single unitary system or two separate independent systems. It is reasonable, therefore, to consider that the similarities in adults' and children's codeswitching patterns are not coincidental. Rather, along with evidence of their early phonological awareness, vocabulary acquisition, and pragmatic language choices, children's codeswitching provides further support for the Independent Systems hypothesis.

Moreover, the comparison of the adults' and children's codeswitches further strengthens the hypothesis that children's grammars develop into adult grammars in a continuous fashion.[14] Additionally, it provides more evidence that grammatical categories are, to some degree, universal across languages.

4.6.3 Other Implications of Codeswitching

In a study of 115 2.5-year-old simultaneous Spanish-English toddlers in South Florida (US), Ribot and Hoff (2014) asked why bilingual children "sometimes choose to speak in only one of the two languages that they understand" (p. 339). To find answers, they used two methods: parents' self-reports to obtain information about the amount of input children received, and the *Expressive One-Word Picture Vocabulary Test Spanish-English Bilingual Edition to measure the children's receptive and expressive language.* According to self-reports by the parents, the children had received different amounts of each language, depending on the household. Ribot and Hoff found that the language used more in the household was the children's stronger language and the one they were more likely to switch into for responses. Accordingly, they noted that children who had heard less Spanish were more likely to codeswitch and give an English response to a Spanish question. But, when spoken to in English they were less likely to switch and respond in Spanish. Therefore, Ribot and Hoff proposed, the reason switching occurred more often from Spanish to English and less from English to

Spanish may be due to the fact that the children received more input in English than they did in Spanish.

Moreover, results from the children's responses to the receptive test showed that the children who codeswitched to English had higher *expressive* vocabulary scores in English than in Spanish.[15] However, remarkably, there was no difference in these children's English and Spanish *receptive* language scores: they understood English and Spanish equally well, but chose to respond in English even when spoken to in Spanish. Additionally, they found that when children were more balanced in their expressive and receptive skills across both languages, they did not codeswitch as much.

A few studies which have looked at children ages five and up show similar results: the language heard less will naturally be the language used less, and therefore the child will have a more limited vocabulary in that language, which in turn produces less expressive capabilities.

We should also consider a few other reasons for the asymmetry in switching by younger children. Many researchers have proposed that the toddler may choose words from the language that has fewer syllables and fewer complicated sounds over a longer, phonologically harder word of the same meaning in the other language. For example, universally, regardless of language, production of the sounds 'l' and 'r' aren't mastered until five to six years of age, in contrast to 'p', 'm', 'n', 'w', 'h', which are mastered by 2.5–3 years of age. Although most of the sounds in English and Spanish overlap, there are some that are exclusive to Spanish such as 'ñ' and trilled 'r', which are not mastered until age six. It is possible that when a bilingual Spanish-English two-and-a-half -year-old has to choose between the word *baby* and *niña* ('baby'), they will produce the phonologically simpler word *baby*.

Context can also encourage codeswitching. It is not uncommon for the language in which events take place to trigger codeswitching, as will contexts in which when some of the words needed may only be known in one of the child's languages. For example, if the child is asked what they did in school that day, the response may very well be in English, if they are attending a school in which English is the language of instruction and other activities.[16] Naturally, the many hours spent hearing and using English (versus the home language) will enhance the child's expressive skills in English.

4.6.4 Codeswitching by Older Children

It's important to remember that codeswitching is maintained by children even after both languages have been fully developed. It is also important to remember that there are no cases reported by parents, researchers, or teachers of children using only code-mixed speech. Just as bilingual adults codeswitch for a variety of reasons, so do children. Recall our discussion of the functions of codeswitching, including the language-identity link in Chapter 3. Once in school, aside from some vocabulary deficiencies due to lack of exposure in the home, children's motivations include codeswitching to either the status language or the heritage language to evoke solidarity, to distance themselves or exclude others, to reaffirm belonging, intimacy, and inclusion, and to establish or wield power within interpersonal relationships with their peers. As we discussed in Section 3.3, Jørgensen (1998), in his study of Turkish-Danish bilingual second, third, and fifth graders, observed that the children codeswitched, mostly intersententially, while working in small groups to complete a task. He also noted that the children used Danish to talk about their assigned task, while Turkish was used to make other personal, non-task related comments. For example, swearing and other insulting or critical comments were made in Turkish, to keep the remarks private. But they also codeswitched to signal a change in the topic of conversation or to evoke unity. Jørgensen concluded that for the children, like with adults, codeswitching was a discourse strategy used to wield power over each other in some cases, while in other instances, they codeswitched to signal solidarity within their interpersonal relationships with each other.

4.7 The Bilingual Child and Language Maintenance

Related to codeswitching among older children is the question of maintenance of the home language. So far, we've considered some of the main issues and outcomes of infants brought up in bilingual households. But what happens when the bilingually raised child enters school? One of the questions frequently asked is whether children will be able to maintain their home language. As with bilingual language acquisition and development, the child's language maintenance depends on a number of variables. As we discussed in Chapter 2, maintenance of multiple languages, in general, requires support from within and from outside the bilingual community. This requirement holds for the individual child's ongoing bilingualism as well. For children, the most crucial factor in home language maintenance is their continued perception that the language spoken at home is essential to their lives. Recall we read earlier about a choice some families make toward that end, namely, exclusively using and insisting the family only uses the heritage language at home; the child is thus encouraged to maintain the home language in order to maintain a strong family bond. Of course, community and institutional support are also critical for maintaining the home language and heritage, as they signal recognition of and respect for the speakers and their heritage. In many bilingual communities, we find cultural centers, language classes, and activities which promote the communities' heritage and history. Availability of various types of media in the home language is also important—an option not readily available to all groups due to costs. These external supports are especially critical to bilingual communities' ongoing survival when bilingual education is not available.

Thinking Matters

Consider the following scenarios:

Scenario 1: Child A has been raised bilingually in a household where each parent consistently uses only his or her language with the child (one-parent one-language method). One of the languages is the majority language. The other is a minority language of the refugee community to which the family belongs and is strongly connected to through social and religious events. At six years of age she'll start kindergarten, which will be taught in the majority language.

Scenario 2: Child B has been raised bilingually by parents who speak both languages to each other and to her. The child's grandmother, who only speaks the minority language, also lives with them. Once she is six, she will also be starting kindergarten in the majority language.

Given what you have read in this chapter and Chapter 2, how well do you think each child will do maintaining their home language? Explain your answer.

4.8 Summary

Although much remains to be investigated in the area of bilingual language acquisition, we now know that many developmentally, the timelines and linguistic achievements of bilingually raised children are on par with that of children raised monolingually:

- In the area of sound perception, no significant differences have been found between monolingual and bilingual infants that might disfavor bilingual language exposure. In fact, studies have shown that bilingual infants continue to make distinctions that monolingual infants cease to make at certain ages, and they maintain certain acquisition strategies such as attention to mouths, beyond that of monolingual children.
- Concerning the acquisition of words, any differences in bilingual toddlers' and young children's vocabulary size when compared to monolingual same-age children are equalized when total numbers of words across both languages are calculated for bilinguals.
- Additionally, bilingually raised infants are immune to notions of mutual exclusivity for object names, a cognitive flexibility that monolingually raised children are not able to cultivate until much later in their development. Therefore, although we do not precisely know if there are any cognitive costs or advantages for bilingually raised infants as they grow, we do know that they are not delayed or hampered in reaching developmental milestones.
- Moreover, bilingually raised children have the undeniable advantage of knowing two languages and being part of two cultures.

As research in this area continues, we need to keep in mind that our pursuit of answers to how bilingual acquisition proceeds should be conducted as good science, untainted by personal, social, and political agendas. John Edwards aptly remarks,

> It is the responsibility of researchers to lay the irrational fears of bilingualism and multilingualism to rest through good science. It is equally important that bilingual and multilingual researchers address socio-political issues head-on.
>
> (Edwards 2013, p. 47)

Initiatives such as the Harmonious Bilingualism Network (HaBilNet), under the supervision of Annick De Houwer and her team (www.uni-erfurt.de/projekte/mehrharmoniehabilnet/), and the Cambridge Bilingualism Network (sites.google.com/site/cambiling/home?authuser=0) are excellent resources for parents and teachers who wish to understand, develop, and promote bilingualism with their children and students.

Discussion Questions

1. How does the Unitary Language System theory differ from the Independent Language System theory? What evidence has been found in support of each?
2. What were some of the early conclusions about childhood bilingualism and its effects on language and cognitive development as compared to children raised monolingually? Why do you think these reports were critical of bilingualism and showed negative results?
3. In your opinion, what are the advantages of raising children bilingually? Are there any disadvantages socially, academically, or cognitively?
4. Why is it important to maintain heritage languages? What are the advantages? Are there any disadvantages to maintaining a heritage language?
5. If you had the opportunity to raise a child bilingually, would you do so? Explain your reasoning.

Projects

1. Create a survey using the five questions posed at the beginning of the chapter. For each question, interview three bilinguals and three

monolinguals and write down their answers. Compare the responses you received for each question to answer the following questions:

(a) How similar were the responses given by the monolingual respondents?

(b) How similar were the responses given by the bilingual respondents?

(c) Did you find any similarities across the monolingual and bilingual responses?

2. Look at these videos of bilingual children using both of their languages. How well do the videos match what you've read about child bilingualism? Is there a difference between comprehension and production? Explain your observations.

www.youtube.com/watch?v=ABpi3gd5ym0—4-year-old bilingual child.

www.youtube.com/watch?v=fJPAJAYSX8A—2-year-old bilingual child.

3. Look for community centers in your town which are linked to a specific culture (such as the Irish American Heritage center in Chicago, the Iranian Society of Colorado, or the Vietnamese Cultural Center in Des Moines, Iowa). See how many different cultural centers you can find.

4. Visit one of the centers you found in (3). What do they provide for their community (e.g., language classes, festivals, performances)?

Notes

1 Carroll comments, "In a critical review, I voice reasons for scepticism that quantity or quality of exposure alone will explain findings. Central constructs are not well defined; inappropriate research methods have been used; the right kind of data is not discussed. Crucially, authors prevaricate on the notion of language itself, switching between cognitive and environmental perspectives. Both are needed to interpret bilingual behaviours but play different roles in the construction of learner grammars." (Carroll, 2017, p. 3)

2 Houston-Price, C., Nakai, S. (2004). Distinguishing novelty and familiarity effects in infant preference procedures. *Infant and child development.* Vol. 13, Issue 4, 341–348. 22 September 2004 https://doi.org/10.1002/icd.364.

3 Studies such as those conducted by Hoff, E., Core, C., Place, S., Rumiche, R., Señor, M., & Parra, M. (2012). Marchman et al. (2004), Conboy and

Thal (2006), and Simon-Cereijido and Gutiérrez-Clellen (2009), Kovács & Mehler, (2009); Petitto, Katerelos, Levy, Gauna, Tetrealt & Ferraroi, (2001), Petitto & Kovelman (2003) and Werker & Byers-Heinlein (2008), among others, provide support for the Independent Language System Hypothesis.

4 Antonella Devescovi, Maria Cristina Caselli, Daniela Marchione, Judy Reilly, Bates, E.n (2003). A Cross-Linguistic Study of the Relationship between Grammar & Lexical Development. Technical Report CND-030. Project in Cognitive and Neural Development Center for Research in Language, University of California, San Diego.

5 Onomatopoetic words are expressions that imitate the sound associated with an animal, object, or action. Each language has its own set of onomatopoetic words. For example, Chinese dogs say wang-wang and not woof-woof.

6 See Tenenbaum et al. (2015) in the references. Their study of monolingual infants' attention to speakers' mouths during speech is directly relevant to the differences found between monolingual and bilingual language acquisition strategies.

7 For example, a 'b' sound is physically articulated with both lips brought together for an instant, and the sound 'o' requires the lips to be rounded during articulation, and so on.

8 Studies conducted by Bialystok et al., 2012; Kroll and Bialystok, 2013, Valian, 2015; Bialystok, 2017; Poarch and Van Hell, 2017; Poarch, 2018; Poarch and Bialystok, 2015 (among others) show positive effects on the executive functions of bilingually raised children.

9 Studies conducted by Duñabeitia, Hernández, Antón, Macizo, Estévez, Fuentes, and Carreiras, 2014; Antón et al., 2014; Gathercole et al., 2014 (among others) show no executive function differences between multilingual and monolingual children.

10 For more details, look for Cummins, J. (1978). *Bilingualism and the Development of Metalinguistic Awareness*. Sage Publishers, 9(2): 131–149. doi.org/10.1177/002202217892001.

11 Cromdal, J. (1999). Childhood bilingualism and metalinguistic skills: analysis and control in young Swedish-English individuals. *Applied Psycholinguistics*, 20, 1–20.

12 See De Houwer's critique of this often politically charged assumption (2009).

13 A much-discussed issue in first language acquisition is whether adult grammars are a continuation of children's grammars or if the two are separate systems. The similarities found between adults' and children's codeswitches may have bearing on this question and on the notion of language universals.

14 One of the ongoing debates in language acquisition is whether children have and operate with a separate grammar (including phonology and morphology) from the adult grammar. The debate is between *continuous* and *discontinuous* systems and revolves mostly around syntax: are adult

grammars a continuation of children's grammars (continuous theory) or is
a child's grammar and children's grammars a completely different set of
rules (discontinuous theory)?

15   They used a self-report method to establish the amount of input children
received from each language and what percentage of time the children
produced conversational codeswitching from Spanish to English and from
English to Spanish.

16   This is also true of adult bilinguals.

References and Recommended Readings

Baum, S. (1997). Early bilingual language acquisition: A sociolinguistic
perspective. In *Proceedings of Salsa V*. (pp. 89–100). Austin, TX: Texas
Linguistic Forum.

Bialystok, E. (2017). The bilingual adaptation: How minds accommodate
experience. *Psychological Bulletin*. 143: 233–262.

Bialystok, E., Craik, F.I.M., & Luk, G. (2012). Bilingualism: Consequences
for mind and brain. *Trends in Cognitive Sciences*. 16: 240–250.

Bilingual/Codeswitching Data. childes.talkbank.org/access/Biling/.

Bosch, L., & Sebastián-Gallés, N. (2001). Evidence of early language
discrimination abilities in infants from bilingual environments. *Infancy*.
2(1): 29–49.

Brownell, R. (2001). *Expressive One-Word Picture Vocabulary Test—Spanish-
English Bilingual Edition*. Novato, CA: Academic Therapy Publications.

Byers-Heinlein, K., Morin-Lessard, E., & Lew-Williams, C. (2017). Bilingual
infants control their languages. *Proceedings of the National Academy of
Sciences*. 114(34): 9032–9037.

Carroll, S. (2017). Exposure and input in bilingual development. *Bilingualism:
Language and Cognition*. 20(1): 177–192.

Conboy, B., & Thal, D. (2006). Ties between the lexicon and grammar: Cross-
sectional and longitudinal studies of bilingual toddlers. *Child Development*.
77: 712–735.

Cummins, J. (1978). Bilingualism and the Development of Metalinguistic
Awareness. *Journal of Cross-Cultural Psychology*. 9(2): 131–149.

Cromdal, J. (1999). Childhood bilingualism and metalinguistic skills:
analysis and control in young Swedish-English individuals. *Applied
Psycholinguistics*. 20: 1–20.

De Houwer, A. (1990). *The Acquisition of Two Languages from Birth: A Case
Study*. Cambridge, UK: Cambridge University Press.

De Houwer, A. (2009). *Bilingual First Language Acquisition*. Bristol, UK:
Multilingual Matters.

Edwards, J. (2013). Multilingualism: Some central concepts. In: Bhatia, T., & Ritchie, W. (Eds.), *The Handbook of Bilingualism and Multilingualism*, 2nd edition. Malden, MA: Blackwell Publishers, Ltd.

Fantini, A. (1985). *Language Acquisition of a Bilingual Child*. San Diego, CA: College Hill Press.

Fennell, C., & Byers-Heinlein, K. (2014). You sound like Mommy: Bilingual and monolingual infants learn words best from speakers typical of their language environments. *International Journal of Behavioral Development*. 38(4): 309–316.

Frank, M.C., Vul, E., & Johnson, S.P. (2008). Development of infants' attention to faces during the first year. *Cognition*. 110(2): 160–170.

Genesee, F. (1989). Early bilingual development: One language or two? *Journal of Child Language*. 6: 161–179.

Goodenough, F. (1926). Racial differences in the intelligence of school children. *Journal of Experimental Psychology*. 9: 388–397.

Hoff, E. (2006). How social contexts support and shape language development. *Developmental Review*. 26: 55–88.

Hoff, E., Core, C., Place, S., Rumiche, R., Señor, M., & Parra, M. (2012). Dual language exposure and early bilingual development. *Journal of Child Language*. 39(1): 1–27.

Houston-Price, C., Caloghiris, Z., & Raviglione, E. (2010). Language experience shapes the development of the mutual exclusivity bias. *Infancy*. 15(2): 125–150.

Johnson, E., & Zamuner, T. (2010). Using infant and toddler testing methods in language acquisition research. In: E. Blom, & S. Unsworth (Eds.), *Experimental Methods in Language Acquisition Research*. Language Learning & Language Teaching, Vol. 27 (pp. 73–94). Philadelphia, PA: John Benjamins Publishing Company.

Jørgensen, J.N. (1998). Children's acquisition of code-switching for power-wielding. In: P. Auer (Ed.), *Codeswitching in Conversation: Language Interaction and Identity* (pp. 237–258). London, UK: Routledge.

Köppe, R., & Meisel, J. (1995). Code-switching in bilingual first language acquisition. In: Milroy, L., & Muysken, P. (Eds.). *One Speaker, Two languages: Cross-disciplinary Perspective on Code-switching* (pp. 276–301). Cambridge, UK: Cambridge University Press.

Kroll, J.F., & Bialystok, E. (2013). Understanding the consequences of bilingualism for language processing and cognition. *Journal of Cognitive Psychology*. 25: 497–514.

Lanza, E. (1997). Language contact in bilingual two-year olds and code switching: language encounters of a different kind? *The International Journal of Bilingualism*. 1(2): 135–162.

Leopold, W. (1939–1949). *Speech Development of a Bilingual Child: A Linguists Record* (vols I–IV). Evanston, IL: Northwestern University Press.

Lewkowicz, D.J., & Hansen-Tift, A.M. (2012). Infants deploy selective attention to the mouth of a talking face when learning speech. *Proceedings of the National Academy of Sciences.* 109: 1431–1436.

Mahootian, S. (1993). A null theory of codeswitching. Ph.D. dissertation, Northwestern University.

Marchman, V.A., Martínez-Sussmann, C., & Dale, P.S. (2004). The language-specific nature of grammatical development: Evidence from bilingual language learners. *Developmental Science.* 7: 212–224.

Mougeon, R., & Beniak, E. (1991). *Linguistic Consequences of Language Contact and Restriction: The Case of French in Ontario, Canada.* Oxford, UK: Clarendon Press.

O'Neill, M. (1998). Support for the independent development hypothesis: Evidence from a study of Russian-English bilinguals. *BUCLD 22 Proceedings.* 586–597.

Peal, E., & Lambert, W.E. (1962). The relation of bilingualism to intelligence. *Psychological Monographs: General and Applied.* 76(27): 1–23.

Poarch, G.J. (2018a). Multilingual language control and executive function: A replication study. *Frontiers in Communication.* 3(46): 1–11.

Poarch, G.J. (2018b). How the use and control of multiple languages can affect attentional processes. In: N. Mani, R.M. Mishra, & Huettig, F. (Eds.), *The Interactive Mind: Language, Vision and Attention* (pp. 53–60). Basingstoke, UK: Macmillan.

Poarch, G.J., & Bialystok, E. (2015). Bilingualism as a model for multitasking. *Development Review.* 35: 113–124.

Ribot, K.M., & Hoff, E. (2014). "¿Cómo estas?" "I am good." Conversational code-switching is related to profiles of expressive and receptive proficiency in Spanish-English bilingual toddlers. *International Journal of Behavioral Development.* 38(4): 333–341.

Ronjat, J. (1913). Le développement du langage observé chez un enfant bilingue. Paris: Champion.

Sebastián-Gallés, N. (2010). Bilingual language acquisition: Where does the difference lie? *Human Development.* 53: 245–255.

Simon-Cereijido, G., & Gutiérrez-Clellen, V. (2009). A cross-linguistic and bilingual evaluation of the interdependence between lexical and grammatical domains. *Applied Psycholinguistics.* 30: 315–337.

Singh, L., Fu, C.S.L., Tay, Z.W., & Golinkof, R.M. (2018). Novel word learning in bilingual and monolingual infants: Evidence for a bilingual advantage. *Child Development.* 89(3): e183–e198.

Tenenbaum, E.J., Sobel, D.M., Sheinkopf, S.J., Malle, B.F., & Morgan, J.L. (2015). Attention to the mouth and gaze following in infancy predict language development. *Journal of Child Language.* 42 (6): 1173–1190.

Valian, V. (2015). Bilingualism and cognition. *Bilingualism: Language and Cognition.* 18: 3–24.

Volterra, V., & Taeschner, T. (1978). The acquisition and development of language by bilingual children. *Journal of Child Language.* 5: 311–326.

Weikum, W.M., Vouloumanos, A., Navarra, J., Soto-Faraco, S., Sebastián-Gallés, N., & Werker, J.F. (2007). Visual language discrimination in infancy. *Science.* 316(5828): 1159.

Yow, Q.W., Tan, J.S.H., & Flynne, S. (2018).Code-switching as a marker of linguistic competence in bilingual children. *Bilingualism: Language and Cognition.* 21(5): 1075–1090.

Chapter 5

Bilingualism and the Brain

As we discovered in Chapter 4, research is ongoing regarding the effects of bilingualism on the child's developing brain and to date, much evidence has surfaced in support of the positive effects of bilingualism. Furthermore, many of the fears associated with childhood bilingualism have been put to rest: bilingualism is not a disability; it does not cause language delay, stuttering or semilingualism. In fact, research indicates that the infant's brain is prepared to accept input from multiple languages and to maintain the languages as separate linguistic systems.

Continuing from Chapter 4, the questions for this chapter pertain to the relationship between the bilingual's two languages and the further cognitive effects of bilingualism on the adult brain. Specifically, psycholinguists and neurolinguists want to know whether bilingualism brings with it cognitive advantages, e.g., higher IQ, faster problem solving, or increased skills on tasks requiring selective attention. Or might there be a cognitive cost to bilingualism, e.g., slower performance rates on tasks due to the cognitive load (i.e., energy needed for processing; see page 157) from keeping languages separated—repressing one language while using the other? Accordingly, researchers seek answers to the following questions:

- How is language processing affected when two or more languages are present?
- Does processing for both languages happen in the same parts of the brain?

- Is there a difference in language processing between early (in childhood) and late (in adulthood) bilinguals?
- Does bilingualism bring a cognitive advantage to the speaker or a cost?
- How do bilinguals control each of their languages to successfully (a) use each language without interference from the other, and (b) use both languages together, often rapidly and seamlessly, to produce intentional and unintentional codemixing?

To begin, let's note that what we know of the brain's functioning is limited. What we know about the bilingual brain is even more limited. In short, when it comes to the effects of bilingualism on the cognitive functions of the adult brain, the jury is still out. Research results in this area of bilingualism have been more mixed than in other areas of bilingualism, and studies have shown conflicting data on whether bilingualism improves, hinders, or has no effect on cognitive functions. Up until the early 1990s, psycholinguists and neurolinguists mostly relied on various types of timed observational experiments to understand the differences between the bilingual and the monolingual brain.[1] For example, reaction time (RT) experiments were used to measure how long participants take to respond to various language tasks and how these reaction times differ between monolinguals and bilinguals. Over the last 20–25 years, technological advances have tremendously increased our access to the brain-in-action. Brain imaging techniques allow us to see which regions of the brain react to various language stimuli and tasks, and to address some of the questions posed earlier, e.g., the similarities and differences between bilingual and monolingual brains in the storage and processing of language. The main imaging techniques used for this purpose are fMRIs, PETs, and ERPs:

fMRIs—Functional Magnetic Resonance Imaging, a noninvasive method used to map brain activities and regions by measuring neural activity.

PET—Positron Emission Tomography uses a dye which contains radioactive tracers and is swallowed, inhaled, or injected. PET scans provide detailed images of the brain's functions and activity by observing which areas of the brain are using more glucose. The scan records activity in progress.

ERP—Evoked Response Potential measures electrical activity in different regions of the brain brought on by visual or auditory 'events'. ERPs can be used for responses to written and spoken language. Electrical responses are recorded using a noninvasive configuration of electrodes attached to the scalp.

5.1 Methodological Problems

From these and other types of less technology-based experimental measures, researchers hope to arrive at a more accurate map of the linguistic brain and to be able to determine the cognitive costs and benefits of bilingualism. That said, we are still faced with studies that show conflicting results. A closer look at these studies helps to identify some of the overarching reasons behind their varied outcomes and conclusions.

Participant pool and proficiency—It's possible that the inconclusive findings so far may stem from a lack of uniformity in defining the subject population and a shortage of adequate numbers of participants (of the same age, socioeconomic status, gender, education, and so on) to allow for useful generalizations. As we learned in Chapter 1, bilingualism is not easily defined: there is no single definition that adequately describes all bilinguals. Moreover, depending on the discipline and researchers carrying out bilingualism studies, we can expect further differences in the criteria used to select subjects, thus making it more difficult to compare results and arrive at definitive conclusions. Though it seems trivial at first blush, how to collect and interpret data depends a lot on which researchers from which fields are conducting the research, even when the questions being asked are the same. A critical part of any research for both scholars and students is to have clear and empirically motivated methods of data collection, including clear definitions of the subject population under study. Unfortunately, the same terminology is too often used differently in different fields. Case in point: in the field of neuropsychology, the most commonly *assumed* definition of a bilingual has been individuals who know and use two languages with equal proficiency, and bilingualism as the equal and active use of both languages, though as we've learned, a more realistic subject population is one with a range of proficiencies across their languages.

Continuum—Another factor that can skew results is the mistaken assumption by many outside of the field of linguistics that bilingualism is a static binary achievement involving two languages—either you are bilingual or you are not. Without making the many distinctions among types of bilingualism that we learned about in Chapters 1–4 (e.g., early or late bilinguals, simultaneous or sequential, passive or active), research results will tell an incomplete story. Attention to these differences is particularly relevant when the study aims to determine the effects of bilingualism on the mature brain. Though there has been more attention given to these and other influential factors in the last half dozen years, much of the earlier research did not adequately screen bilingual participants.

Numbers—A further factor is that many reported results are based on a very small number of participants, some as few as three. Though not a deal breaker in and of itself, combined with other factors, generalizing the results of smaller studies is less reliable.

Language-internal differences—A further potential complication is that of merging cross-linguistic results. Though absolutely essential to understanding the cognitive effects of bilingualism, combining or comparing results from the same tasks performed by bilinguals of different languages may be problematic. For example, the same task performed by Chinese-French bilinguals and French-English bilinguals may yield conflicting results not because of an error in the task or the researchers' methodology but due to the researcher's incomplete understanding of the structural differences (in terms of grammatical rules) between Chinese and English, and the possible processing differences the structural differences may produce.

But all in all, the good news is that our knowledge of the bilingual brain continues to grow due to advances in technology.

5.2 Useful Terminology

So what can we say about the bilingual brain? Before we look at some of the research results, let's familiarize ourselves with a few useful psycholinguistic and neurolinguistic terms and concepts.

Executive functions are the mental processes that allow us to plan, to remember instructions, to focus attention, to multitask, to prioritize tasks, and to filter distractions. From childhood on, the brain's executive functions develop and grow.

Cognitive load is simply the amount of mental energy needed to process information when you hear or see something, especially when it is new information and doesn't already have a 'seat' in your long-term memory. The newer the information, the more energy you need to process it and to funnel it into long-term storage. Processing has two important limitations. First is the fact that the working memory can only hold information for about 10 seconds before the information is either lost, in which case you won't be able to recall it, or processed and sent to long-term memory. Second, working memory can only process five to seven pieces of information at a time. So, for example, remembering six numbers as three pairs of numbers (28 13 97) is an easier task than remembering those same six numbers as six separate numbers (2 8 1 3 9 7). Each pair is one bit of information, so you are required to remember three pieces of information, where the six single digits require you to remember six bits of information. Consequently, the set of two digit numbers takes less time to send to permanent memory and less mental energy to recall.

Neural Activation in psychology refers to the state of attention or wakefulness of various parts of the brain as a response to various types of stimuli. In the context of our discussion, this activation is in response to language and language tasks. Neural activation indicates processing of information. Essentially, the more complex a task, the more neural activation needed to perform the task. For example, repeating a word requires less activation than generating a list of words.

Semantic memory refers to the general knowledge of the meaning of words and concepts which we amass throughout our lives. For example knowing that a hotdog is a food, or that rain refers to weather is part of your semantic memory.

Semantic networks are the interrelationships of words and concepts through meaning (as opposed to the relationship of words based on shared sounds, rhyming, number of syllables, etc.). For example, the word 'fire' has a number of other words closely associated with it semantically. In turn, each of these words has their own meaning relationships with one another and with other words. The diagram in Figure 5.1 is a partial representation of a semantic network involving the word 'fire'.

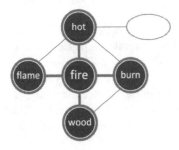

Figure 5.1 Example of a semantic network.

Thinking Matters

Can you expand the 'fire' network in Figure 5.1? What words would you add to 'fire' and to its associated words 'hot', 'flame', burn', and 'wood' to expand the network? Go to www.youtube.com/watch?v=3wMfKTkYemY to see more semantic networks.

Recent breakthroughs in imaging have been able to verify that the anterior temporal lobe, a region just in front of each ear, is the part of the brain responsible for the way we understand words, meanings, and concepts. *The Moth Radio Hour* (a National Public Radio broadcast) aired a story on how functional magnetic resonance imaging (fMRI) was used to measure the brain activity in seven people as they listened to more than two hours of stories.

A compilation of these images shows where and how we store meaning and similar concepts to create semantic networks in the brain: www.youtube.com/watch?v=k61nJkx5aDQ.[2]

5.3 Some Answers

In the next five sections, we review findings from current studies that provide some answers to the questions we posed at the start of this chapter.

5.3.1 Are Bilinguals' Languages Processed in Different or in Overlapping Brain Regions?

The question of whether bilinguals' languages are processed in *separate* regions or *overlapping* regions has been a subject of study for over a century. It is important to distinguish this question from the question regarding whether bilinguals' two grammars are fused together as a single, unitary system, or whether the two grammars are kept as two separate systems. Processing (neural activity) in overlapping regions of the brain does not require the grammars to be a single system.

Early on, a number of aphasia studies found that some bilingual stroke patients had selective impairment of one language but not the other. Consequently, largely based on these reports, it was suggested that bilinguals' two languages are represented and processed in different parts of the brain (Paradis, 1995). Recent fMRI evidence has shed more light on this question. For example, in their study of six fluent Spanish-English early bilinguals who had been exposed to both languages before the age of five, Hernandez, Dapretto, Mazziotta, and Bookheimer (2001) asked participants to perform picture recognition and naming tasks in each of their languages while undergoing an fMRI. The results showed neural activity in overlapping areas of the brain for all six participants. Given the small number of participants, their level of fluency, the narrow scope of the tasks (i.e., only single words were required), and that the same two languages were involved, the authors rightly caution that the results obtained from their study shouldn't be taken as evidence for all bilingual processing:

> Our study used picture naming, a task which is thought to tap into single word production. Hence, it is difficult to establish that this particular task is representative of the entire range of bilingual language processing. There are other tasks that could be used both at the single word level and at the sentence and discourse level.
>
> (p. 518)

Hernandez et al. further suggest that the differences in processing that other studies found, but that were not found in their own study, might stem from the differences in the structure of the languages themselves and are not a by-product of the effects of bilingualism on the brain.

For example, in a study of monolingual English and Italian speakers, Paulesu, McCrory, Fazio, Menoncello, Brunswick, Cappa, and Cotelli (2000) found overlaps as well as differences in the neural activation regions between the two groups during reading tasks in their respective languages. It was hypothesized that these differences in neural activation could be due to the fact that Italian, unlike English, marks gender (feminine/masculine) on its articles, nouns, and adjectives. For example, in English there is no difference in the form of the article or adjective whether we say 'a tall woman' or 'a tall man'. In Italian, however, the article 'a' and the adjective 'tall' have different forms when combined with the word 'man' than when combined with 'woman'. Feminine words typically end with 'a', so their articles and adjectives must also end with 'a', while masculine words end with 'o' as do their articles and adjectives: *una donna alta* is 'a tall woman', where *un uomo alto* is 'a tall man'.

Hernandez et al. suggest that these seemingly small differences between Italian and English may require activating a different part of the brain for each language. Therefore, it may not be the effects of bilingualism that cause activation in a different region of the brain for the English-Italian bilingual but the nature of Italian itself vis-à-vis English that calls for a different type of processing. Other studies have also found differences in activation regions when examining the perception of tone by monolingual Chinese, Thai, and English speakers (Gandour, Wong, Hsieh, Weinzapfel, Van Lancker, & Hutchins, 2000).

Still other studies show that overall, *fluency* and age of acquisition (i.e., whether the speaker is a *late* or *early* bilingual) are factors in neural activation. More-fluent bilinguals needed less processing time (neural activation) in performing language tasks in both of their languages than did less-fluent bilinguals.

In addition to the contributions these studies make to our pool of knowledge about the bilingual brain, what they tell us is that before we can definitively answer the questions of whether and how exposure to two languages affects the brain's language processing, we have many more questions to answer.

5.3.2 Can Early Exposure to Two Languages Affect Processing?

An equally important line of research pursued by psychologists and neurolinguists is the extent to which early bilingual language exposure does or does not affect language processing. In other words, we want to know the extent to which neural activation patterns in early bilinguals differs (or does not differ) from that of late bilinguals and monolinguals. Anatomical studies which look at the structure of the brain have noted an increase in bilinguals' grey matter as compared to that of monolinguals (grey matter processes information in the brain and is involved with muscle control, seeing, hearing, memory, emotions, speech, decision making, and self-control[3]), suggesting that the bilingual brain is structurally different from the monolingual brain. Moreover, comparison of early and late bilinguals shows more grey matter in the brain of early bilinguals than that of late bilinguals. Consequently, these findings have led researchers to conclude that the brain changes with long-term exposure to more than one language.

Other evidence that supports the possibility that bilingualism can lead to changes in brain structure and cognitive systems comes from studies in second language learning. Li, Legault, and Litcofsky's (2014) comprehensive literature review of the structural and cognitive effects of bilingualism found consistent differences in the white and grey matter structure of the brain between monolinguals and bilinguals participants, even those who had had short-term periods of second-language learning.

The results of these studies, taken together with findings from bilingual infant and adult studies, have prompted researchers to ask whether the structural changes and differences in amount of grey matter are an outcome of *language processing* differences between monolinguals and bilinguals. In search of more answers to this question, Kovelman, Baker, and Pettito (2008) reasoned that neural activation may very well differ between bilinguals and monolinguals. In their study, they investigated whether bilinguals process language differently than monolinguals of the same language when interacting in monolingual mode (using only one of their languages). Relatedly, they asked whether there are fundamental differences in the way bilinguals process language as compared with that of monolinguals. To find answers to these questions, they presented 11 early "highly proficient" Spanish-English bilinguals and 10 English monolinguals with a sentence judgment task in which participants had to judge the grammaticality of sentences while undergoing fMRIs. The same sets of sentences were given to both bilingual and monolingual groups. The bilinguals were given the sentences in Spanish and in English, while monolinguals were only given the English sentences.

Kovelman et al. predicted two distinct possible outcomes: either bilinguals and monolinguals would show differences in neural activation during the task, or they would not. In the case of the former, differences in neural activation would suggest that monolinguals and bilinguals process language in a different manner from each other; hence, bilingualism would show what the authors refer to as a "neural signature". They summarize their important findings as follows:

> That the bilinguals showed processing differences in English versus Spanish ... lends support to the hypothesis that bilinguals can develop two differentiated, monolingual-like, linguistic systems in one brain. Moreover, the findings offer novel insights into the previously unresolved one "fused" versus two "differentiated" linguistic systems debate in bilingual language processing by discovering evidence that bilinguals have a *differentiated* neural pattern of activation for each language.
>
> (p. 166)

Moreover, Kovelman et al. found that their bilingual participants showed normal language processing in each of their two languages. They concluded that contrary to some educators' concerns that early exposure to two languages might cause long-lasting language confusion, their study provided strong counterevidence to such worries.

Other breakthroughs in neuroscience have made a direct link between experience and changes to brain structure and cognitive processes. Importantly, the human brain has been found to enjoy lifelong 'neuroplasticity', the ability to learn new things and pave new pathways through experience (Pascual-Leone, Amedi, Fregni, & Merabet, 2005).[4] For example, there is evidence that experiences such as musical training, learning Braille, or even juggling can modify the structure of the brain. In a review of research on the effects of bilingualism, Bialystok (2017) evaluates results from studies investigating the relationship between bilingualism, brain structure, and cognition. Overall, these studies covered a wide age range, from infants to children and to young and older adults. Bialystok approaches her evaluation from the perspective of experience-dependent plasticity, a theory based on the neuroplasticity of the brain and its ability to restructure itself by developing new neural connections when exposed to new experiences, whether to enable the damaged brain to adjust to injuries, or to allow the healthy brain to adjust to new experiences. In her review, Bialystok reasons that:

> If experience can shape brain structure and cognitive ability, then bilingualism is a prime candidate for such effects. Language use is the most intense, sustained, and integrative experience in which humans engage. The intensity reflects the role that language has in all our activities, not only for verbal communication but also for conceptualizing and interpreting ongoing experience. Semantic networks are invoked each time an event is understood or a memory is formed. Language use is sustained because of all human activities, none consumes the proportion of waking (and perhaps nonwaking) time that language does.

(pp. 233–234)

She further argues that bilingualism can not only modify language processing regions and functions of the brain but can also bring about changes to areas and processes involved with nonverbal processing.

5.3.3 Is There a Cognitive Advantage to Bilingualism in Adulthood?

The answer, in brief is, sometimes for some types of tasks. Recall that from the early 20th century until the early 1960s researchers in the United States believed that bilingualism was a cognitive disadvantage and the source of diminished mental capacities. Later, bilingualism was associated with poor performance in school along with other intellectual and cognitive difficulties. In recent decades, we have learned more about the cognitive effects of bilingualism, although as noted in the introduction to this chapter, results have been mixed, in part due to methodological inconsistencies across the various studies. In order to gain a clearer understanding of the effects associated with bilingualism, four researchers, Adesope, Lavin, Thompson, and Ungerleider (2010) conducted a sweeping review of 63 published studies on various aspects of the cognitive effects of bilingualism, which altogether

involved a total of 6,022 participants. The authors compiled and analyzed the data from these studies, coding for the following:

- Grade and age level—The 6,022 participants ranged from pre-
  kindergarten children to adults with post-secondary education.
- Languages spoken by the bilingual participants—The lan-
  guages paired with English included Chinese, Arabic, French,
  Tamil, Italian, Urdu, Cantonese, Mandarin, Russian, German,
  Spanish, Greek, Pidgin, Catalan, and Serbian. A few other
  pairs were also present: Catalan-Spanish, Cantonese-Mandarin,
  German-French, and Russian-Hebrew, Armenian-Persian, and
  Turkish-Persian.
- Positive or negative cognitive effects—These included executive
  control, meta-linguistic awareness, verbal and non-verbal problem
  solving, working memory, attentional control, mutual exclusivity, phonological processing, syntactic processing, correcting and
  explaining grammatical errors, and solving math problems.

At the end of their analysis, Adesope et al. conclude the following:

> Although monolingualism is often depicted as normative, the best
> available evidence indicates that, around the world, bilingual and
> multilingual speakers outnumber monolingual speakers (Tucker,
> 1998). The current work suggests that bilingualism (and, presum-
> ably, multilingualism) is associated with a number of cognitive
> benefits. These findings point to the need for further work investi-
> gating the utility of these benefits in a variety of contexts.
>
> (pp. 230–231)

In step with the Adesope et al.'s report, Bialystok, Craik, and Luk
(2012) reviewed more than 100 studies which used behavioral and
neuroimaging methods to examine the effects of bilingualism on
cognition in adulthood and to explore possible mechanisms for these
effects. They were specifically interested in reports of bilingual
advantages in executive control. In their review, they found a pattern
of better executive control by bilinguals at all ages when compared to
monolinguals of the same age and to other comparable demographic
variables.

As we learned earlier, executive control and functions are the set of skills needed to multitask, problem solve, maintain focus, and control impulses. Executive functions develop from shortly after birth through young adulthood and begin to decline in old age. In children, executive control is central to academic achievement. Bialystok et al.'s review notes that research has found that bilinguals' enhanced cognitive functions continue in older bilingual adults and protect the brain against cognitive decline for an average of three years longer as compared to monolingual adults. They conclude that bilinguals' "lifelong experience in managing attention to two languages reorganizes specific brain networks, creating a more effective basis for executive control and sustaining better cognitive performance throughout the lifespan" (p. 240). They conclude that bilingualism has a somewhat muted effect in adulthood generally but a larger role in older age specifically, protecting against cognitive decline, a concept known as "cognitive reserve".

Socio-economic status (SES) is one of the variables many researchers take into account in cognitive development studies. SES has also become a consideration in bilingualism studies. In her recent review of studies on bilingualism and cognition, Bialystok (2017) states that while some have argued that the advantage bilingual children have demonstrated on executive function tasks can be attributed to SES and not bilingualism, many other studies have found no correlation between SES and bilingual advantage. Specifically, studies have found that monolingual children and adults from a high socio-economic class do not perform better than bilingual children and adults from high or low socio-economic classes. Conversely, bilingual children and adults from low socio-economic classes outperform monolingual children and adults in both low and high socio-economic classes (e.g., Blom, Küntay, Messer, Verhagen, & Leseman, 2014; Engel de Abreu, Cruz-Santos, Tourinho, Martin, & Bialystok, 2012; Kang, Thoemmes, & Lust, 2016; Nair, Biedermann, & Nickels, 2017; Morales, Calvo, & Bialystok, 2013; Yang, Yang, & Lust, 2011).

Bialystok also observes that still others have unsuccessfully tried to pin bilinguals' cognitive advantage to immigration. For example, she notes that some researchers (e.g., Fuller-Thomson, 2015; Fuller-Thomson, Milaszewski, & Abdelmessih, 2013) argue that the bilingual advantage is due to the "healthy immigrant" phenomenon, i.e., that those who immigrate are also those individuals who are more likely to succeed under challenging circumstances. She counters their arguments that bilinguals' cognitive advantages are an outcome of immigration, and notes,

> [T]he predictions from this view are not supported by analyses that divide the sample according to immigration status (Schweizer, Craik, & Bialystok, 2013) nor by close examination of the logic of the argument and the existing data (Bak, 2015; Bak & Alladi, 2016). More broadly, effects of bilingualism found in countries where bilingualism is not associated with immigration, such as India (Alladi et al., 2013) and Spain (Costa et al., 2008) are equivalent in nature and degree to effects found in countries where bilinguals are more likely to be immigrants.
>
> (Bialystok, 2017, p. 251)

In sum, the answer to our question of whether there is a cognitive advantage to bilingualism in adulthood is a qualified 'yes'. Through advances in technology and a better understanding of bilingualism in general, we have been able to discard many of the negative conclusions from earlier studies. In their place, we've brought in new evidence of the cognitive benefits of bilingualism throughout the lifespan.

5.3.4 Are Both Languages Activated at All Times?

Whether bilinguals' languages are activated at all times is yet another unresolved question. A number of studies have concluded that there is some degree of activation of both languages and interaction between the two languages of fluent bilinguals at all times, even in seemingly monolingual contexts. The studies provide evidence through the results from **priming tasks** and **lexical decision tasks**.

Priming—The priming effect was first employed by psycholinguists in 1971 to plot out neural connections and relationships across concepts and words. Priming is a psychological technique which can reveal relationships between and across words, concepts, and perceptions. Priming effects can result from linguistically, conceptually, or perceptually related stimuli. The simple science behind priming is that, without conscious control, one stimulus can influence a response to a following stimulus. For example, priming can occur from hearing a word, or a sound, or from seeing, smelling, or touching something. For instance, given the priming word 'fork', the word 'spoon' is recognized more quickly than the word 'doctor'. The explanation is that a fork is semantically and conceptually more closely associated with a spoon than with a doctor. Thus, in a mental semantic network, 'fork' and 'spoon' are more directly linked than are 'fork' and 'doctor'. Hence 'spoon' is more quickly activated than 'doctor' (see semantic networks for 'spoon' and 'doctor' in Figure 5.2).

Lexical decision tasks—These tasks can also be used to examine speakers' conscious and tacit knowledge of their language(s). One common lexical decision task is a simple yes-no task where speakers are asked to judge whether a series of sounds or letters is a word or a non-word. These types of experiments are easily adapted and used with bilingual participants in order to help gauge the relationship between their languages, including whether both languages are also activated. For example, participants are given a series of related words in one language which then speeds up (i.e., primes) retrieval of related words in the other language. Or subjects may be asked to decide whether a string of letters *could* be a word in one language. For example, can n-o-p be a word in English? Yes. Why? Because the combination of the sounds n-o-p does not violate any of the sound grouping rules of English. Conversely, the combination d-n-o-p cannot be a word of English, because 'dn' combinations are not allowed at the beginning of words in English.

By measuring bilinguals' response times in priming and lexical decision tasks in each of their languages, some researchers have

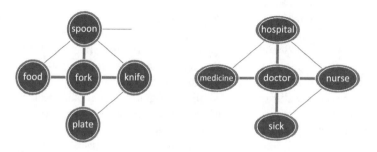

Figure 5.2 Semantic networks for the words 'fork' and 'doctor'.

concluded that, though the participants are only working in one language, the other, unused language nonetheless influences response times and decisions. This, in turn, suggests that both languages are always activated even when only one language is in use. However, it is worthwhile to consider that none of these studies guarantees that the participants are not *already primed* when they come in to take part in these laboratory experiments. If the participants have been recruited because they are bilingual, chances are they are aware well before the experiments begin that whatever they are asked to do will likely involve their two languages. Also, recall that in Section 5.3.3 we learned that recent studies show that fluent bilinguals may have overlapping semantic regions in their brains. So although the languages are separate systems, neural activity occurs in the same regions for some language functions. It is, therefore, not a surprise that the concept of *fire* may have the English word *fire* and the Persian word *atesh* ('fire') stored and accessed in the same region—in other words, that neural activity for the word in English is in the same region as for the word in Persian.

To learn more about and see some demonstrations of priming, go to the YouTube videos listed after this paragraph. The first explains priming in the context of language, including bilingualism. In the second video, Dr. Michael Shermer, columnist for Scientific American, demonstrates priming and word recognition using Led Zeppelin's *Stairway to Heaven*. In the third video, magician and mentalist Derren Brown demonstrates priming in a larger sensory context.

- www.youtube.com/watch?v=NGrxUp0pvVo
- www.youtube.com/watch?v=79KO1q3ND6g
- www.youtube.com/watch?v=EUA4Q5aoG74

Mahootian and Schott (2017) also investigated the effects of bilingualism on cognitive functions, seeking answers to the following questions: (i) Are bilinguals' languages in simultaneous activation? (ii) Does bilingualism result in additional cognitive load for the speaker? (iii) Does age of exposure to each language affect the answers to (i) and (ii)? The study, conducted over a year-long period, was in two parts: a *digit span task* and a *Stroop effect task*. For both tasks, bilinguals performed a language **match trial** (the task was given in English, and the participant responded in English) and a language **switch trial** (the task was given in English and the participant responded in Spanish). We posed two hypotheses:

Hypothesis 1: Bilinguals' two languages are simultaneously activated, producing a cognitive load. In this case, the bilingual participants will take longer to respond in both the match and switch trials during both the digit span and Stroop effect tasks, as compared to monolinguals.

Hypothesis 2: Bilinguals' two languages are not in simultaneous activation. In this case, bilingual participants will (a) perform just as well as monolinguals by giving the same numbers of correct answers in the same amount of time when directions and responses are in the same language, and (b) when the task language and the response language differ from each other, bilinguals will not perform as well (they will make more errors and/or take longer to respond), due to the time needed to activate the other language during both the digit span and the Stroop effect task.

Learn more about the digit span task and the Stroop effect task. Then try the suggested websites to test your own skills with the Stroop effect before reading Mahootian and Schott's results.

Digit span task: Commonly used by psychologists to measure cognitive load, a digit span task involves participants repeating a series of numbers in the same order in which they heard them. In the Mahootian and Schott study, participants were required to repeat back in the same order a series of five single-digit numbers (e.g., 7, 2, 5, 9, 3). If participants performed this task successfully, they were given a longer list, up to nine numbers. The length of the longest list a person is able to repeat correctly is that person's digit span. In our study, the task was given orally to monolingual English speakers and bilingual English-Spanish speakers. There were two versions of the task for the bilingual participants: (1) directions were in English, and participants were asked to repeat the numbers in Spanish, (2) directions were in English, and participants were asked to repeat the numbers in English.

Stroop effect task: Named after the psychologist John Ridley Stroop, the Stroop effect assesses selective attention capacity, processing speed, and cognitive flexibility. The basic idea is to name the color a color word is printed in, ignoring the word itself. For example, if the word RED is written in BLUE INK, you need to say 'BLUE'. Stroop test results show that people can accurately and quickly read color words no matter what color the words are printed in. But when the they are asked to identify the color of the ink and bypass the written name, they experience problems, taking longer to respond and making errors.

Neuroscientist Bryn Farnsworth explains why the errors and slow-downs happen (imotions.com/blog/the-stroop-effect/):

> What this reveals is that the brain can't help but read. As habitual readers, we encounter and comprehend words on such a persistent basis that the reading occurs almost effortlessly, whereas declaration of a color requires more cognitive effort. When there is a conflict between these two sources of information, our cognitive load is increased, and our brains have to work harder to resolve the required difference. Performing these tasks (preventing reading, processing word color, and resolving information conflict) ultimately slows down our responses and makes the task take longer.

Go to this website to learn how the Stroop effect works and to try it for yourself:

Science World—www.youtube.com/watch?v=InoHIdIUe3Y
Demonstration of Stroop effect—www.math.unt.edu/~tam/SelfTests/ StroopEffects.html.
Mythbusters—www.youtube.com/results?search_query=stroop+ effect

The results showed that when switching between English and Spanish was not required, early bilingual participants do not perform differently from their English monolingual counterparts during language tasks. However, they did not perform as well as monolinguals when a language switch was involved. We concluded that the results suggest bilinguals' languages are not always simultaneously active, contrary to previously held assumptions (Colome, 2001; Van Hell & Dijkstra, 2002; Michael & Gollan, 2005). The study is explained in some detail below.

Participants, recruited through fliers on a university campus, comprised faculty, staff, and students. The fliers, some in Spanish and some in English, asked for bilingual Spanish-English speakers and monolingual speakers interested in taking part in a memory task. Participants included 17 adult bilingual Spanish-English speakers and 18 adult monolingual English speakers.

After arriving at the test site but before the start of the tasks, participants were asked to self-identify as bilingual or monolingual. Directions for both tasks were pre-recorded. Upon completing both tasks, participants filled out a demographic survey. Bilingual participants were given a longer survey which included questions about age of exposure to each language, the contexts in which each language is used, and frequency of use of each language (such as how often and with whom they used each language, how often they read, watched TV, listened to music, and so on, in each language). They were also asked whether they would choose to raise their children bilingually. Bilinguals were given the option to complete the survey in either of their languages. All chose the English version of the survey.

The purpose of giving the demographic and language-use survey after the task (instead of before) was to minimize any unintentional priming effect (such as activation of both languages) if a subject believes both languages will be involved in the tasks before starting the task. Based on the demographic information, the bilingual participants' results were then divided into two groups of early and late bilinguals: 10 of the participants had been exposed to both languages between birth and age 5, and seven between the ages of 10 and 15. Results from both the Stroop effect and the digit span tests, regardless of age of exposure to the second language, strongly indicated that bilinguals' two languages are not simultaneously activated, contrary to previous reports (Colome, 2001; Van Hell & Dijkstra, 2002; Michael & Gollan, 2005).

5.3.5 Does Switching Between Languages Have a Processing Cost? Or Does Switching Enhance Executive Functions?

Studies in this area have been inconclusive, with some showing that codeswitching involves aspects of executive functions, and therefore, increases general executive processing time and puts extra demands on cognitive control (Hernandez et al., 2001). Other studies, however, have failed to find any significant differences in executive function during codeswitching. Of course, it's possible that the results are not as contradictory as they may appear. How? Recall the discussions regarding methodology and the importance of comparing apples to apples: depending on participants' languages, their age, gender, socioeconomic status, education, etc., and the particular tasks they are asked to perform will naturally produce a variety of results. Some studies may show that bilinguals possess enhanced executive control for spatial reasoning, while other tasks may show no difference between monolinguals' and bilinguals' executive control functions on a different task. In a recent review of current studies, Blanco-Elorrieta and Pylkkänen (2018) found that, in fact, intentional switching by bilinguals reduces previously recorded cognitive processing loads associated with switching, or even eliminates them. That said, the authors suggest that the advantage often associated with bilingualism based on bilinguals' ability to easily switch between languages may be characteristic of those bilinguals who switch regularly due to conversational contextual needs. They further suggest that switching may only be costly under certain conditions and under certain "communicative demands", with the conclusion that switching is "not inherently effortful".

Clearly, there is much more to learn about the effects of codeswitching on cognitive functions. For now, we can entertain all possibilities. The main point to remember is that regardless of whatever cost may be involved, codeswitching is a natural part of bilingualism. It is rule-governed and systematic, and it is part of the dynamic and discursive behavior of every bilingual speech community.

5.4 Summary

Our knowledge of the adult bilingual brain is continually increasing. Recent technological advances have allowed researchers to peer into the brain as it performs various language tasks, providing a deeper understanding of the brain in general as well as of the processing similarities and differences between monolingual brains and bilingual brains. These studies have confirmed that the brain is multilingually capable at various ages. They have also helped to confirm that factors such as age of acquisition and the amount of exposure to each language can determine how much the bilingual's languages may affect each other during processing and to what extent the neural activities of the two languages may occur in overlapping areas in the brain.

In terms of specific answers to the big question of cognitive advantages or costs, as with studies of child bilingualism, we face mixed results from the research on adult bilinguals. While some research has shown evidence of positive cognitive effects in processing, others have found no cognitive advantage, and still others have suggested that bilingualism may have some possible processing costs. In the latter cases, the "cost" is in terms of incremental cognitive load and processing time, neither of which affect individuals' actual academic, intellectual, and social abilities and accomplishments. The positive cognitive effects seem to be an enhancement of the bilingual's ability to exercise executive control, meaning that he or she is able to minimize distractions and to more easily stay on task. Bilingualism seems to also have benefits for the older brain, staving off effects of language loss due to Alzheimer's, up to an average of three years. Without doubt, everyone is on the same page and unreservedly agrees that one of the greatest benefits of bilingualism may very well be sociocultural, allowing speakers to be part of multiple cultures and speech communities.

Projects

1. *Semantic networks*: Find four participants with the same educational background and close to the same age: two who self-assess as fluent bilinguals of the same two languages, and two monolinguals (of the same language). One of the languages of the bilinguals must be the same as that of the monolinguals (for example,

all four must speak English). Either individually or as a group (make sure they are sitting far apart from each other), ask them to make a list in their shared language of as many words as they can related to the word 'crime'. Set a timer for one minute. Once completed, gather the lists. Next, have them do the same task but with words that begin with 'P'. Collect their lists at the end of the task. Count the words in each task for each of the participants. Did the monolinguals produce more, less, or the same number of words as the bilinguals? You can repeat this by substituting the noun 'crime' with another noun or different parts of speech, for instance, an adjective (yellow, tall, cold, etc.), adverb, or verb. What results do you predict? Why? What results did you get? Did you get different results in terms of the number of words produced by monolinguals as compared to bilinguals?

2. *Develop your own research proposal*: Based on what you have learned, work in pairs or groups of three to develop a research proposal that you think would provide more answers to the questions posed in this chapter and in Chapter 4. Make sure your proposal includes the following information with a section head for each: major question(s) and hypotheses, methodology, equipment (including recording equipment), subject population, and how you will recruit the participants (through flyers, social media, in person, etc.).

Watch These Videos To Learn More about the Brain and Cognition

Steven Pinker: Linguistics as a Window to Understanding the Brain
www.youtube.com/watch?v=Q-B_ONJIEcE

Anatomy of the Brain
www.mayfieldclinic.com/PE-AnatBrain.htm
www.health24.com/Mental-Health/Brain/Multimedia/Transparent-
    brains-20130418.
www.youtube.com/watch?v=kMKc8nfPATI

Cognition: How Your Mind Can Amaze and Betray You.
www.youtube.com/watch?v=R-sVnmmw6WY

Memory

www.youtube.com/watch?v=bSycdIx-C48

visual.pearsoncmg.com/mypsychlab/index.html?clip=1&episode=
    episode03

What is a neuron and what does it do?

visual.pearsoncmg.com/mypsychlab/index.html?clip=1&episode=
    episode03

Notes

1 This area of research is mostly under the purview of psycholinguists and neurolinguists. As you may recollect from Section 3.2 of Chapter 3, psycholinguists, by and large, tend to use experimental approaches. Study participants are observed as they perform tasks in laboratory settings. Linguists tend toward observational methodologies, where natural speech in natural contexts is observed and recorded. Though both methods have obvious merits, and the best of all worlds is when the answers are sought through both approaches, when trying to determine which regions of the brain are involved in various activities, observation in natural settings will not yield any insights.

2 For more details of the study, see the related paper "Natural speech reveals the semantic maps that tile human cerebral cortex", by Alexander G. Huth, Wendy A. de Heer, Thomas L. Griffiths, Frédéric E. Theunissen & Jack L. Gallant. *Nature.* 532: 453–458 (28 April 2016).

3 www.news-medical.net/health/What-is-Grey-Matter.aspx

4 Neuroplasticity and positive effects of enriching experience in rats have been known for over seven decades (Hebb, 1949), but effects on the human brain are a recent discovery, owing to the imaging technologies now available.

References and Recommended Readings

Adesope, O., Lavin, T., Thompson, T., & Ungerleider, C. (2010). A systematic review and meta-analysis of the cognitive correlates of bilingualism. *Review of Educational Research.* 80(2): 207–245.

Bak, T.H. (2015). Beyond a simple "yes" and "no". *Cortex.* 73: 332–333.

Bak, T.H. (2016). The impact of bilingualism on cognitive aging and dementia: Finding a path through a forest of confounding variables. *Linguistic Approaches to Bilingualism.* 6: 205–226.

Bak, T.H., & Alladi, S. (2016). Bilingualism, dementia and the tale of many variables: Why we need to move beyond the Western World. Commentary on Lawton et al. (2015) and Fuller-Thomson (2015). *Cortex.* 74: 315–317.

Bialystok, E. (2017). The bilingual adaptation: How minds accommodate experience. *Psychological Bulletin.* 143(3): 233–262.

Bialystok, E., Craik, F.I.M., & Luk, G. (2012). Bilingualism: Consequences for mind and brain. *Trends in Cognitive Science.* 16(4): 240–250.

Blanco-Elorrieta, E., & Pylkkänen, L. (2018). Ecological validity in bilingualism research and the bilingual advantage. *Trends in Cognitive Sciences.* 22(12): 1117–1126.

Blom, E., Küntay, A.C., Messer, M., Verhagen, J., & Leseman, P. (2014). The benefits of being bilingual: Working memory in bilingual Turkish-Dutch children. *Journal of Experimental Child Psychology.* 128: 105–119.

Costa, A., Hernández, M., & Sebastián-Gallés, N. (2008). Bilingualism aids conflict resolution: Evidence from the ANT task. *Cognition.* 106: 59–86.

Engel de Abreu, P.M., Cruz-Santos, A., Tourinho, C.J., Martin, R., & Bialystok, E. (2012). Bilingualism enriches the poor: Enhanced cognitive control in low-income minority children. *Psychological Science.* 23: 1364–1371.

Gandour, J., Wong, D., Hsieh, L., Weinzapfel, B., Van Lancker, D., & Hutchins, G.D. (2000). A crosslinguistic PET study of tone perception. *Journal of Cognitive Neuroscience.* 12: 207–222.

Hebb, D.O. (1949). *The Organization of Behavior: A Neuropsychological Theory.* New York, NY: Wiley and Sons.

Hernandez, A.E., Dapretto, M., Mazziotta, J., & Bookheimer, S. (2001). Language switching and language representation in Spanish–English bilinguals: An fMRI study, *NeuroImage.* 14: 510–520.

Hernandez, A.E., Martinez, A., & Kohnert, K. (2000). In search of the language switch: An fMRI study of picture naming in Spanish–English bilinguals. *Brain and Language.* 73(3): 421–431.

Huth, A.G., de Heer, W.A., Griffiths, T.L., Theunissen, F.E., & Gallant, J.L. (2016). Natural speech reveals the semantic maps that tile human cerebral cortex. *Nature.* 532: 453–458.

Kang, C., Thoemmes, & F., Lust, B. (2016). Effects of SES on executive attention in Malay–English bilingual children in Singapore. *Bilingualism: Language and Cognition.* 19: 1042–1056.

Kovelman, I., Baker, S.A., & Petitto, L.A. (2008). Bilingual and monolingual brains compared: a functional magnetic resonance imaging investigation of syntactic processing and a possible "neural signature" of bilingualism. *Journal of Cognitive Neuroscience.* 20(1): 153–169.

Li, P., Legault, J., & Litcofsky, K.A. (2014). Neuroplasticity as a function of second language learning: Anatomical changes in the human brain. *Cortex.* 58: 301–324.

Mahootian, S., & Schott, S. (2017). The effects of bilingualism on performance of cognitive tasks: Evidence against simultaneous language activation in bilinguals. *The Second Biennial International Convention of Psychological Science (ICPS)*, Austria Center Vienna, Vienna, Austria.

Morales, J., Calvo, A., & Bialystok, E. (2013). Working memory development in monolingual and bilingual children. *Journal of Experimental Child Psychology*. 114: 187–202 .09.002.

Morales, J., Gómez-Ariza, C.J., & Bajo, M.T. (2013). Dual mechanisms of cognitive control in bilinguals and monolinguals. *Journal of Cognitive Psychology*. 25: 531–546.

Morton, J.B., & Harper, S.N. (2007). What did Simon say? Revisiting the bilingual advantage. *Developmental Science*. 10: 719–726.

Nair, V.K.K., Biedermann, B., & Nickels, L. (2017). Effect of socio-economic status on cognitive control in non-literate bilingual speakers. *Bilingualism: Language and Cognition*. 20(5): 999–1009.

Paradis, M. (Ed.). (1995). *Bilingual Aphasia 100 Years Later: Consensus and Controversies*. Oxford, UK: Pergamon.

Paulesu, E., McCrory, E., Fazio, F., Menoncello, L., Brunswick, N., Cappa, S.F., & Cotelli, M. (2000). A cultural effect on brain function. *Nature Neuroscience*. 3: 91–96.

Peristeri, E., Tsimpli, I.M., Sorace, A., & Tsapkini, K. (2018). Language interference and inhibition in early and late successive bilingualism. *Bilingualism: Language and Cognition*. 21(5): 1009–1034.

Schweizer, T., Craik, F.I.M., & Bialystok, E. (2013). Bilingualism, not immigration status, is associated with maintained cognitive level in Alzheimer's disease. *Cortex*. 49: 1442–1443.

Yang, S., Yang, H., & Lust, B. (2011). Early childhood bilingualism leads to advances in executive attention: Dissociating culture and language. *Bilingualism: Language and Cognition*. 14: 412–422.

Chapter 6

Summary

Referring to the results of their own study, Hartshorne, Tenenbaum, and Pinker (2018) write the following:

> [F]uture work that successfully addresses the limitations of the present study may similarly prompt significant revisions in what we believe to be true. Science is the process of becoming less wrong, and while hopefully the revisions are smaller and smaller after each step, there is no way of knowing that this is the case in advance.
>
> (p. 275)

Their claim holds true for all academic work and should be wholeheartedly embraced by researchers in all fields. In this volume, I have tried to present, synthesize, and summarize the key points and issues in the study of bilingualism. Obviously, many fuzzy and gray areas remain, but we have a good start. Defining bilingualism goes hand in hand with understanding what it means to be bilingual. Over the last nine decades, many descriptions have been proposed to capture the many facets of what has become an important part of the field of linguistics. As an interdisciplinary field, the study of bilingualism provides us with insights into every aspect of language and language use, from models of language structure and discourse, to a deeper understanding of language acquisition, brain structure and cognitive functions, to language policy and curriculum building. Given that bilingualism is the norm rather than the exception, continued research in this exciting cross-disciplinary area offers us the opportunity to understand the human brain, our system of communication, and its relationship to our identities and cultures at the individual and community levels. It further allows us a different window through which to understand the linguistic capabilities of infants.

We started our discussion by defining bilingualism as the regular use of two or more languages in everyday contexts, one that is best described on a continuum, where the speaker's languages can shift in dominance from one topic to the next, and from one situation or interlocutor to the next. We discovered that this somewhat open-ended, dynamic framework allows for an integration of the many factors which intersect and give way to bilingualism, whether in infancy or in adulthood, through home, education, or work, as immigrants, or as the colonized. And though we've come a long way from thinking about bilingualism as detrimental to mental health and cognitive development, and from viewing codeswitching as an ungrammatical mish-mash, we are still far from understanding all of the variables and processes which result in individual bilingualism.

Our review of attitudes towards bilingualism and codeswitching revealed an intersection of attitudes towards immigration, race, and ethnicity that erroneously deny the natural and positive properties of bilingualism. Codeswitching was discussed in terms of its discourse functions as well as its universally rule-governed structure. We also examined motivations behind language choice and how the bilingual's choice of language can impact a conversation to create distance or intimacy, assert authority and status, or create solidarity with other speakers. The discussion of codeswitching functions led us to examine the relationship between language and identity. We considered the use of mixed code in popular media as a means to signal a shift in the status of a community and its speakers, or to highlight the presence of a minority group. Altogether, we determined that intentional use of mixed code in publications can perform four discourse functions: as a political statement of defiance; as a call for globalization and deterritorizing of identities and borders; as a statement and indicator of the shift in social status and, therefore, power; and finally, as a symbol of ethnicity and emerging hyphenated communities. Moreover, we examined the less acknowledged yet important notion of cultural codeswitching among speakers of nonstandard varieties, and the pressure experienced by members of some minority communities to codeswitch to the standard variety.

We also learned that bilingualism is not always a sustainable outcome of language contact. Given that language contact has itself been a by-product of war, conquests, immigration, and global economies, language loss and death are too often an outcome of contact. Recent efforts to document and revitalize endangered languages are finding some success in different parts of the world, including among native languages in the Americas.

We've discovered that infants raised bilingually develop strategies to distinguish and manage their languages as early as their eighth month of life, and as they grow into toddlers, develop metalinguistic awareness (the ability to talk about language, monitor and analyze it as a system of rules, sounds, etc.). Our knowledge of the functions and structure of the bilingual brain, from infancy to old age, has also grown. Greatly assisted by advances in medical technologies such as fMRIs, PET scans, and ERPs over the last three decades, we are able to watch the brain in action as it solves problems and manages multiple tasks. Through neurological and behavioral studies, we have been able to learn more about the structure and cognitive functions of the brain and its potential for adaptability through experience. We have come to know that bilingual brains do, in fact, operate differently from monolingual brains, structurally and in neural activity. We have also seen that for some functions, monolingual and bilingual brains show no distinctions. Ultimately, the areas that stand out for future research are the realms of psycholinguistics and neurolinguistics, because what we learn about the bilingual brain will tell us more about the functions and structure of the brain as a whole.

> [B]ilingualism is a positive adaptation to the environment, beyond increased communicative competence in a second language and greater cultural understanding. For bilingual parents who are contemplating whether to teach their children more than one language, the message is clear. Bilingualism can be a valued precursor of general as well as lingual flexibility (…), second language experience can change structural and functional properties of the mind.
> (Randsell, Arecco, &
> Levy, 2001, p. 113)

References

Hartshorne, J.K., Tenenbaum, J.B., & Pinker, S. (2018). A critical period for second language acquisition: Evidence from 2/3 million English speakers. *Cognition*. 177: 263–277.

Randsell, S., Arecco, M.R., & Levy, C.M. (2001). Bilingual long-term working memory: The effects of working memory loads on quality and fluency. *Applied Psycholinguistics*. 22: 113–128.

Appendix

The switch approach is a lexical acquisition testing method used with older infants. It has two phases, a teaching phase and a switch phase. In the teaching phase, infants are taught two new words, or more specifically, researchers use two made-up words in order to be certain the infants have never heard the words before. The infants are presented with two objects on a computer screen. At the same time that they see the objects, the infants hear the made-up word associated with each object. The object-word association phase continues for a few moments until the infant gets bored (no longer looks at the screen). At this point, the switch phase begins. As the term implies, a switch takes place. Here, the switch is between the word and the object: object one is shown while the word for object two is heard. The prediction is that infants who have learned the new words from Phase 1 will detect a mismatch between the word and the object and will look at the anomalous, switched pairs longer than when the correct words are presented with the images.

Fennel and Byers-Heinlein (2014) used this method to measure the effects of bilingualism on vocabulary development. Their study included two groups of 1.5-year-olds. Half of the babies were growing up in bilingual French-English households, while the other half were from monolingual English-speaking households. They sought to determine whether monolingual and bilingually raised toddlers perform equally when learning new words where only the initial consonants are different (e.g., 'fit' and 'bit'). The example that Fennel and

Byers-Heinlein give is of a crown moving back and forth on the screen while the infant is hearing the word 'kem', and a molecule made of building blocks is shown while they here 'gem'. The object-word association phase continues for a few minutes until the infant gets bored (no longer looks at the screen). At this point, the switch phase begins, where the label for the two objects is switched so that object one is presented on the screen while the word for object two is being heard. The prediction is that the infants who have learned the two new words presented in Phase 1 will look at the anomalous, switched pairs longer than when the correct labels are presented with the images, thus indicating they had learned the two new words.

Reference

Fennell, Christopher, & Byers-Heinlein, Krista. (2014). You sound like Mommy: Bilingual and monolingual infants learn words best from speakers typical of their language environments. *International Journal of Behavioral Development*. 38(4): 309–316.

Index